THE

PEDIGREE OF THE DEVIL.

THE

PEDIGREE OF THE DEVIL.

BY

FREDERIC T. HALL, F.R.A.S.

𝔚𝔦𝔱𝔥 𝔍𝔩𝔩𝔲𝔰𝔱𝔯𝔞𝔱𝔦𝔬𝔫𝔰.

ARNO PRESS
A New York Times Company
New York • 1979

First published London, 1883
Reissued 1971 by Benjamin Blom, Inc.
Reprint Edition 1979 by Arno Press Inc.
LC79-89808
ISBN 0-405-08594-X
Manufactured in the United States of America

PREFACE.

EVERYTHING has a pedigree. Everything, whether animate or inanimate, whether a thing of sense or a creation of the mind, every idea whether based on fact or the growth of a delusion, every truth and every error, has its pedigree.

A pedigree is a line of ancestors, a chain of causes and effects, each link first an effect and then a cause. Rarely, if ever, is an effect the result of an isolated cause, but causes cross and interlace in such endless combinations, that novel effects are continually being produced.

The simplest facts have endless pedigrees of causes and effects. A pebble lying on the path appears a simple object, commonplace and uninteresting ; but let the geologist unfold its pedigree, and trace it down from the rock of which it was originally part, at a time when our planet was a barren lifeless mass of matter, and when it did not contain even the most elementary form of life ; following this little

lump of matter through all the convulsions of Nature,
the vicissitudes of climate, the development of vege-
table and animal life, and the thousand circumstances
which have contributed to the reduction of that
pebble to its present form and nature, and determined its present situation, and we find a mass of
causes and effects widening out in the retrospect
with bewildering complication.

And so with each living animal, lines of ancestors
multiplying as they recede into antiquity in geome-
trical proportion, until the ancestry seems to include
the whole world of Nature, and involve all beings in
one vast cousinship ; always exposed to vicissitudes
of climate, food, and the endless other incidents of
the great struggle for existence, ever at work, modi-
fying the characteristics of each race, evolving new
forms and making fixity of type impossible.

Idea and ideals have also their pedigrees ; but the
ancestor ideas are not so easily dissected as those of
material facts.   Still ideas and ideals are facts, none
the less so, that they may have been imaginary and
false.   An idea is a fact although a mere figment of
the brain, founded on a fallacy ; and when an idea
becomes an article of faith, it becomes so strong a
fact that it will be the parent of a thousand other
ideas, each in its turn the father of a thousand
others.

Amongst ideas, that of the Devil may rank as one which has taken a powerful hold on the mind of man. The present volume is directed to an examination of some of the many causes which have contributed to the construction of the ideal Devil.

It is difficult to discriminate with accuracy all the links which have formed the direct lines of descent, as each link in its turn has been a centre of radiation, a point of departure for other conceptions. It has been necessary to examine some of these collateral branches, in order to illustrate the process of divergence and point out some of the collateral relationships; and indeed the temptation to digress is great. But this has been done as little as possible, the object being, not to dogmatize on the result, but to examine the origin of a single but complex ideal, and the stages by which the result is connected with the original germs.

The Devil treated of is the modern orthodox Devil of Christian Belief. No attempt is therefore made to discuss the ideals and personifications of evil realized by other creeds, except so far as light may seem to be thrown on the history of the Christian Devil.

As to the conclusions to which the facts may point, it is for each to form his own opinion. The existence or non-existence of the Devil, his personality or abstract existence, are not the questions treated of in these pages : an ideal of the Devil has existed, and still exists, and the only object is to trace the origin and evolution of that ideal.

Amongst the numerous works from which I have drawn materials for the pedigree, I would mention those of Mr. E. B. Tylor, Mr. Moncure Conway, M. François Lenormant, and the late Mr. Keightley, all of which have been of great assistance to me. I have endeavoured as far as possible to acknowledge in foot-notes the authorities from which I have drawn ; where I may not have done this, I still would express my indebtedness to those authors whose works I have used.

F. T. H.

Moore Place, Esher,
November, 1882.

CONTENTS.

IV.

V.

IX.

THE DEVIL.

WHAT is understood by " The Devil " ?

This question, apparently so simple, is nevertheless most difficult to answer. The difficulty arises from the multifarious and vague notions which at all times have been, and still are, held upon the subject, even by those from whom critical precision might fairly be expected. Comparatively few, however, have examined the subject : it is not deemed in itself an attractive one, and those who would enter upon the inquiry are open to the charge of either meddling with unwholesome subjects, or treading upon dangerous ground.

The term " devil " has enjoyed a very wide range of application, but, according to the most generally received notion, a devil is a spirit of Evil, and " The Devil " is the personification of supreme Evil. There have, in the human mind, been conceived as many devils as there have been ideas of evil ; and the trooping legions of evil thoughts have naturally suggested legions of devils, legions have suggested leaders, and these have involved a supreme head ; so

B

that a Supreme Devil, the Spirit of Supreme Evil, has been realized. Had there not been the idea of a Supreme God, there would certainly not have been the idea of a Supreme Devil. The two ideas of good and evil are, in fact, inseparable, and logically dependent upon one another : we cannot conceive shade, except as contrasted with light, nor death except as following life : so, were there not such an idea as that of goodness, evil would be inconceivable : every vice is the opposite of some virtue, and every evil the opposite of some good : the idea of a Supreme God has paved the way for that of a Supreme Devil.

II.

EVIL.

Definition of Evil—Personal Evil—Social and Domestic Evil—
National Evil—Theological and Religious Evil—Savage, Bar-
baric, and Civilized Moral Standards—Intolerance—Evil is
"Opposition."

WHAT then is Evil?

Anything is evil which is opposed to good. But, what is Good? Good is almost as indefinable; like evil, it only exists relatively: it certainly does exist in the mind of each reasonable being, but the idea of goodness varies with the standard formed by each individual thinker. Each age, each nation, each creed, each sect, each man, woman and child has had a standard of goodness different from any other: the tree, which of all others has borne the greatest variety of fruits, is the tree of the knowledge of good and evil.

Evil then is simply a question of standard. Whatever *I* consider to be evil, is *my* evil, and whatever *I* believe to be good, is *my* good. If I am uncontrolled by social and national ties, I enforce my standard to the utmost of my power, and everything that is

B 2

opposed to me is evil. I wish to eat and drink, and it
is good that I should eat and drink : anything that
prevents my obtaining food, is an evil : the ground
is barren and unfruitful, and I curse it as an evil ;
the desert wind dries up all moisture, bringing no
pregnant clouds, nor cool refreshing dews ; the sun
looks down relentlessly from a brazen sky, Nature
groans in drought ; and I curse the desert wind, the
sky and sun as unmixed evils. At last the clouds
appear, darkening the horizon, advancing with swift
but solemn pace, until they shroud the wide expanse
of heaven with deep impenetrable gloom : the mut-
tering thunder swells into deafening peals, as earth
and heaven exchange their lightning volleys ; at last
the monsoon bursts ; the thirsty ground drinks in
the copious rain ; languid Nature revives on
every side ; the frowning storm, with all its welcome turmoil, sails on, and flocks of fleecy clouds,
drawn up from each valley, follow in its train ; while
sounds of rippling waters, answering the songs of
birds, waken glad Nature to new life :—I, refreshed,
sink into sweet repose, the crisis past, and hope again
restored.   The storm, the rain, even the thunder and
the lightning, are my good : for they have brought
nothing but peace and plenty to me and mine.   But
that lightning has struck down my neighbour's roof-
tree, and killed his cattle ; the deluge of rain has
swept in an inundating flood over his most fruitful

field, taken with it his prospect of a plenteous harvest, and left gaunt ruin in its wake :—the storm is his evil, and as such he curses it.

The frost, the snow, the glacial winter of the North, grip Nature by the throat, causing there as much desolation as the desert wind under the tropical sun. The dwellers in the north regard the frost and the cold biting winds as unmitigated evils ; and yet the world of Nature would be poorly off, and dwellers in warmer climes would indeed have reason to cry out, were frost and glacial winds cut out of Nature's scheme.   The Lapps and Eskimos may well worship the Sun, and welcome him as their best friend, as he delivers them from the bondage of the Frost Giants. What benighted beings they must think those who dread the sunrise !   And yet there are those who look upon the sun as a cruel and relentless enemy.

But natural phenomena are not the only influences which, for good or evil, affect man's struggle for existence : the pestilence stalks through the land, and sweeps whole nations from its surface ; fever and insidious disease creep over thresholds at the dead of night, and carry off the first-born of man and beast ; wolves will decimate the flock, and the roaring lion will prowl about the herd, seeking whom he may devour, and not in vain ; monsters of uncouth shape and dire resistless strength have, in times gone by, levied their tax of blood on man and beast, reducing all to abject terror; until arose some hero, who, by conquering the common enemy, has earned immortal fame, and lived a demigod : or the locust-swarms will sweep through a land, like " the garden of Eden before them," and nought but a "desolate wilderness behind them," and earn title to the symbol of destruction,[1] and a quasi-deification through the terror they inspire.[2] No wonder that all these opposing influences, enemies to man's well-being, should be classed by him as evils.

But man has more than food and raiment to seek, more than his own life to protect and prolong. He has social and domestic ties : the family, the clan, the tribe and the race cling together for mutual support and protection, not only in face of natural obstacles, but also of other men, engaged, like themselves, in the restless struggle for existence. Amongst themselves, a standard of social and domestic good is formed, assented to, and enforced by the majority, and probably handed down from generation to generation as a rule of life, departure from which is evil. Each set of rules, so framed, grows and is modified from time to time to meet the needs of the community for which it was framed. Similar sets are framed for other communities : but

---

[1] The Scythians were spoken of as a cloud of locusts.—Joel ii. 3.

[2] " Abaddon," locusts, is given as a synonym of " Apollyon " and the angel of the bottomless pit.—Rev. ix. 11.

these all by degrees diverge in meeting the varied wants and circumstances of each, until in time they become so opposite, that what is good according to one standard, may be downright evil according to another. Hence the pride of race, and the prejudice of caste : artificial standards of good, cause artificial evil ; as society becomes more complex, the former becomes more stringent and the latter more heinous ; and that which in all good faith was instituted for a good purpose, becomes the vehicle of evil; that which was intended for life brings death.[1] A law is made to obviate an evil, the law is glossed and over-laden with tradition, and the original good of the law is far outweighed by the evil it has brought about. Such are the laws of race and caste : the Brahman who dare not give a drink of water to the dying Pariah, lest he should become defiled, and be put back in the scale of rising life : the Hebrews enjoined to put away their Gentile wives and children, on pain of excommunication :[2] the white American, who to this day, while shedding his life-blood in the cause of negro emancipation, and preaching the universal brother-hood of man, dreads the most distant family alliance with a man of colour, for fear of social degradation.

---

[1] " The commandment which was ordained to life, I found to be unto death."—Rom. vii. 10.

[2] One hundred and thirteen wives, many with families, are re-corded as put away by command.—*See* Ezra x. and Neh. xiii. 25.

All these are subjected to social and domestic laws, once made no doubt for good, but which have long been producing more evils than they remedied.

As families and races became blended into national communities, and the relations between man and man became more complex still, fresh standards had to be created of national and political good. In forming such standards, the majority of power in the State enforced its views on the minority. It was possible that the rule for the whole family might not coincide with the views of some individuals of it, and that the rule for the clan or tribe might involve a still greater mass of difference of opinion : but when a code of laws had to be framed for a whole nation, it is certain that individual opinions would be more divided still. A man might honestly follow the dictates of his conscience, and thus conform to his individual standard of good ; he might fulfil all his social and domestic duties, and thus live up to the standard of the family and race ; and still be banned as a criminal, exiled as an outlaw, or shot down as a traitor, for disobedience to his nation's laws, and for nonconformity to the standard of good, artificially created for the general welfare and safety of the nation. It is not difficult to understand that it may be quite right for a man to fight in the army of the nation to which he belongs, and that it should be a crime punishable with death for him to pass over to the opposing army, and fight with them against his own countrymen; but this crime could only exist for political reasons, and might be the result of a mere accidental circumstance :—whether the man were born on this or that side of a little stream :—the Alsatian who fought against France in 1870, was a traitor to his country ; the inhabitant of Alsace who should now fight with France against Germany, would be as much a traitor as the other : although perhaps, in each case, a true and blameless man in every other relation of life.

There is however one field, which has been more fruitful than all others put together, in the creation of evil, by the erection of standards of good ; and that is the wide, far-stretching field of Theology and Superstition. In the primitive states of society of every epoch, in which men have been banded together in only small communities, where they have found themselves face to face with such physical difficulties, that their main business has been to sustain life, without any attempt to refine existence by culture, a Theology can hardly be said to exist at all ; and the religious sentiment is satisfied by a superstitious dread of the unseen beings who are believed to exercise a baneful influence over Nature, and an unreasoning faith in those who profess a power to influence those beings. In such a stage of society, a sense of moral right and wrong in relation to the unseen world, is not developed : it is purely a question of power : the deity is to be feared and propitiated, because he is more powerful than I am, and will favour me more than my neighbour or my enemy, if I am more assiduous than he is. Where there is, by chance, a beneficent deity, in the pantheon of a nation, it by no means follows that he is as powerful as the malevolent one : and thus it happens that as amongst these men, so with their gods, might is right : Good is what each wishes to have and enjoy, and Evil everything that bars the way and prevents its attainment.

This is and has been the basis of the religion, or rather superstition, of the great mass of the savage population of the world, which has no written history, and next to no traditions, and whose religion, like its language, is as unstable as shifting sands ;—after a few years so changed as to be hardly recognizable. A large proportion of the human race must always have been in this condition, all too uncertain to fix with definite ideas of good or evil.

Other communities which have emerged from the savage state, and entered that of barbarism, have generally had some fixed notions as to good and evil, beyond the mere dictates of the individual fancy. They have some runic poetry, or national songs ; some ritual, or incantation ; something formulated and handed down from generation to generation, which acquires strength as time goes on, and finishes sometimes by becoming the sacred record of a nation, the basis of a faith; in defence of which men will fight, and bleed, and die, with all the devotion of which disinterested human nature is capable. Many of these creeds have lived on down to the present day, and have become embalmed in the sacred books of the most highly civilized nations of the world; others have dropped out of memory, the races who held them have been overwhelmed and dispersed, and the conqueror's creed has ruled with the conqueror's sword. Such barbaric nations have generally acknowledged the power of a world to come, and made the future state dependent upon the present life or mode of death or burial. The standard of goodness has varied through the range of almost every possible idea;—death in battle, or some special mode of burial; the observance of certain forms, sacrifices, or other modes of propitiation, may have constituted the passport to a happy future, with little or no regard to what we should call the moral aspect of the case, beyond the recognition of such primitive virtues as courage and prudent forethought. Some have approached nearer to a moral code; the mere fierceness of the warlike instinct, and prudential measures of a blind superstition, being supplemented by the recognition of such milder virtues as honesty, chastity and veracity, and making them a condition for reward. Nations owning such a code have, however, not long remained barbarian, but have rapidly advanced to the stage of civilization in which, as a rule, the moral virtues have been fully recognized, and supported by all the sanctions of religion.

As no theology has ever been quite independent of mythology, so no religion has ever been quite free from superstition : a theology which discards its mythology is on the eve of melting away : a religion which loses its superstition relaxes its hold on the ordinary human mind, its individuality is effaced, and it dies out and is forgotten. If a religion has vitality, it is necessarily intolerant : it must main-tain that its gods are the only true ones, or at least that they are stronger than those of any other creed ; or, if one god alone be worshipped, then that all other gods are false.   This, the highest refine-ment of the religious idea, produces the greatest amount of antagonism : and, standing on his own high pedestal, its votary regards the whole world as sunk in vice, seething in impurity, steeped in superstition, and that " every imagination of man's heart is only evil continually."[1] Every god but the one true God, every being but his own obedient servants, every man but his own devoted worshippers, is, and must

---

[1] Gen. vi. 5.

be, a malignant enemy ; every idea not sanctioned by the particular code of religion and morality accepted by the particular creed, is evil; and it is the bounden duty of every one to stamp out such evil, at the peril of incurring the same condemnation : " Woe is unto me if I preach not the Gospel."[1]

Evil is " opposition." The savage seeks his food : Nature, the elements, wild beasts and enemies oppose him : they are his evil. He seeks to preserve his comfort and his life, his family and his possessions ; the storm that blasts his home, the pestilence that carries off his children, the wild beast that decimates his flock, the locusts that strip his fields, are all evils. The patriarch ruling over his family or his tribe, makes simple rules for the maintenance of order, and the preservation of the race : some Esau will persist in taking wives of the daughters of Heth, and that perverse opposition to the patriarch's will becomes a social, a domestic evil : the patriarch's successor applies the rule, by compelling 113 men to put away their wives, and discard all their own children, the marriages having been in opposition to the old patriarchal law, and therefore evil.[2] Families grow into tribes, and tribes into nations, which settle down and legislate for mutual

---

[1] i Cor. ix. 16.   [2] See ante p. 7.

protection and security : thousands of laws are embodied in hundreds of volumes to regulate the complex compact of the nation : the problem of right and wrong becomes itself so complex, and so beyond the range of the untrained conscience, that a class of men are specially set apart to devote their lives to solving it, and settling and expounding what is right and wrong ; and none but the more intelligent of the community are able even then to follow out the reasoning : yet, any mistake in this is treated as an opposition to the law, it is an offence, a legal or national evil.

But when we come to deal with the religious or theological element in the world : when we find that the Egyptian considered 166 chapters of ritual neces- sary to protect him from opposing spirits in his pas- sage from earth to heaven, and that he went to the grave literally papered and painted over with his ritual in order to conquer : when we hear of the Buddhist canon comprising 500 monster volumes of instructions how to live in order at last to shake off the trammels of a weary life, and reach the restful haven of " nothingness :" when the Hindu holds that life after life must be passed through with ever in- creasing sanctity, each bristling with minute observ- ances, before the soul can shake off its earthly coil, and merge into the Deity, and rest : when the Jewish Rabbi points to 12 densely printed folio volumes of

Talmudic writing as the rule of life,[1] and makes that rule so difficult to learn aright, that it is heaven's own business to argue over it: and when each Christian sect brands all the other Christian sects as heretics, and the 350 millions of Buddhists, the 150 millions of Brahmanists, and the 180 millions of Mohammedans (to say nothing of his heathen fellow-creatures) as hopeless enemies of truth: when we find that each of these creeds throws back the fatal charge on all the others ; the mass of recognized evil in the world becomes overwhelming to the view :— but, the whole of this evil can nevertheless be summed up in the one single word " OPPOSITION."

Evil then is opposition, and only exists in relation to Good, and the concept of a " Spirit of Evil" partakes of the same relative character.

---

[1] Hershon's "Pentateuch according to the Talmud" iii.

III.

SATAN.

THE devil of the present day is known by the name of Satan ; portrayed by Milton, and brought within the compass of the ordinary human mind. There was a Satan in the Old Testament, but not Milton's : the old Hebrew Satan was either an adversary or an accuser : he was a sort of public prosecutor in the spiritual world, wandering up and down in the earth, spying out men's conduct, weighing their motives, and reporting their failings to Jehovah, the God of all mankind ; taking a grim pleasure in his work, but still fulfilling a necessary office. Man, a sinful, stumbling creature, did not like this vigilant accuser, always lying at the catch to throw the worst colour on his actions, and hold up his sins to the light of heaven : but after all, this Satan was but a public prosecutor on a large scale, and was only different in degree from the policeman who detects and prosecutes the modern thief, and thereby becomes his Satan.

No : our devil is not the Satan of the Hebrews, nor the Asmodeus of the Jews, nor any of the demons of nature or mythology, nor any dethroned god who has seen better days, although he combines many of the characteristics of each of these : but we look in vain amongst them for the unmixed spirit of malignancy which is the central idea of Satan, the modern devil. Christians are the natural successors of the Hebrews in the main features of their creed, but whatever spirits of evil the Hebrews acknowledged, they never realized the existence of a Spirit of malignancy, incapable of good, and only existing for the purpose of creating evil, until they heard of Ahriman the supreme evil spirit of the Persian system. Throughout all the creeds and mythologies of the ancient world, he alone possessed the germ of that which has become the exclusive and distinguishing characteristic of the modern Devil.

The term "Satan" and "Satans" which occur in the Old Testament, are certainly not applicable to the modern conception of Satan as a spirit of evil; although it is not difficult to detect in the old Hebrew mind a fruitful soil, in which the idea, afterwards evolved, would readily take root. The original idea of a "Satan" is that of an "adversary," or agent of "opposition." The angel which is said to have with-

stood Balaam is in the same breath spoken of as
" The angel of the Lord," and a " Satan."[1] When
the Philistines under Achish their king were about
to commence hostilities against the Israelites under
Saul, and David and his men were about to march
with the Philistines ; the latter objected, lest, in the
day of battle, David should become a " Satan" to
them, by deserting to the enemy.[2] When David,
in later life, was returning to Jerusalem, after
Absalom's rebellion and death ; and his lately dis-
affected subjects were, in turn, making their sub-
mission ; amongst them came the truculent Shimei :
Abishai, David's nephew, one of the fierce sons of
Zeruiah, advised that Shimei should be put to death :
this grated upon David's feelings, at a time when he
was filled with exuberant joy at his own restoration ;
and he rebuked Abishai as a " Satan."[3] Again, Satan
is said to have provoked David to number Israel,[4]
and at the same time, that " the Lord moved David
to number Israel :"[5] a course strenuously opposed by
Joab, another of the sons of Zeruiah. Solomon in
his message to Hiram, king of Tyre, congratulated
himself on having no " Satans," and that this peaceful immunity from discord enabled him to build the
Temple, which had been forbidden to his warlike

---

[1] Num. xxii. 22, 32.   [2] 1 Sam. xxix. 4.   [3] 2 Sam. xix. 22.
      [4] 1 Chron. xxi. 1.   [5] 2 Sam. xxiv. 1.

father David.[1]   This immunity was not, however,
lasting ; for Hadad, the Edomite, and Rezon, of
Zobah, became " Satans " to Solomon, after his profuse luxury had opened the way for corruption and
disaffection.[2]   In all these cases, the idea is simply
identical with the plain meaning of the word :
a Satan is an opponent, an adversary. In the
elaborate curse embodied in the 109th Psalm,[3] the
writer speaks of his enemies as his " Satans," and
prays that the object of his anathema may have
" Satan " standing at his right hand.[4] The Psalmist
himself, in the sequel, fairly assumes the office of his
enemy's "Satan," by enumerating his crimes and
failings, and exposing them in their worst light.   In
the 71st Psalm, enemies (v. 10) are identified with
" Satans," or adversaries (v. 13).

The only other places in the Old Testament where
the word occurs, are in the Book of Job, and the prophecy of Zechariah.   In the Book of Job, Satan
appears with a distinct personality, and is associated
with the sons of God, and in attendance with them
before the throne of Jehovah.   He is the cynical
critic of Job's actions, and in that character he ac-
cuses him of insincerity and instability; and receives
permission from Jehovah to test the justice of this

---

[1] 1 Kings v. 4.   [3] Ps. cix. 4, 20, 29.
[2] 1 Kings xi. 14, 23, 25.   [4] Ib. 6.

accusation, by afflicting Job in everything he holds
dear.   We have here the spy, the informer, the
public prosecutor, the executioner ; all embodied in
Satan, the adversary: these attributes are not
amiable ones, but the writer does not suggest the
absolute antagonism between Jehovah and Satan,
which is a fundamental dogma of modern Christianity.

In the prophecy of Zechariah,[1] Satan again, with
an apparent personality, is represented as standing at
the right hand of Joshua, the high-priest, to resist
him : he seems to be claiming strict justice against
one open to accusation; for Joshua is clothed in filthy
garments—the type of sin and pollution.   Jehovah
relents, and mercy triumphs over justice : the filthy
garments are taken away, and fair raiment substituted.   Even here, the character of Satan, although
hard, is not devoid of all virtue, for it evinces a sense
of justice.

The Hebrews before the Captivity seem to have
held no specific doctrine respecting evil spirits; or,
if they did, such doctrine was not in conflict with
that held by other peoples, for no controversy on the
subject is recorded.   When they were carried away
captives to Babylon, they successively came into contact with the Chaldean and Persian elements ; and

---

[1] Zech. iii. 1.

contemporaneous and subsequent writers give evidence of an alteration of conception, both with regard to the personality of a great principle of evil, and to the organization of subordinate evil spirits, or demons. This change of views was not equally rapid along the whole line of thought; but, the germs of new opinions having been implanted, they grew slowly but surely, until they completely overshadowed the original dogma, and created what practically amounted to a new religion.

The Chaldeans or Babylonians believed in the existence of vast multitudes of spirits, good, bad and indifferent, with which the physical and moral universe was peopled, and by which all phenomena of nature, and the events of life, were regulated and influenced. The Hebrews had already a belief in the existence of angels or spirits, whose business it was to regulate the affairs of mankind in obedience to the divine behests. We have appearances of angels to Abraham, Lot, Jacob, Joshua, and others, bringing them assistance : and angels destroying Sodom and Gomorrah, the first-born of Egypt, directing the pestilence in Jerusalem, and slaying the army of Sennacherib : but there is nothing to show that the old Hebrew considered every tree, stone and river, as possessed with its own personal spirit, which might at any moment quit its abode, and exercise a direct influence upon his life and welfare. After the return from the Captivity, however, Jewish thought took a fresh departure, Rabbinical speculations ran riot on the subject of angels and demons, and vied with the Babylonians in their realization of good and evil spiritual beings, interfering with, and regulating, the most trivial events of life : they numbered them by millions and billions, and were accustomed to talk of them as being so numerous and ubiquitous, that, if visible, no one could bear the shock. This idea grew in intensity as time went on, and we find in the text of the New Testament ample evidence of an established belief in the existence of innumerable demons— legions of devils—possessing and tyrannizing over the bodies of men and animals ; and myriads of angels, surrounding the saints, and ministering to them.

Side by side with this belief in the multitude of good and evil spirits, there was slowly growing up in the Jewish mind a belief in a prince of evil, malignant, powerful and successful ; hating Jehovah and all good ; directing the spiritual hierarchy of evil to ceaseless attacks upon Jehovah's works, intimately acquainted with all the foibles of weak humanity, and employing this knowledge for their ruin and destruction. The first prince of the demons was Asmodeus, the demon of fiery and uncontrollable lust. The besetting sin of the nation, impurity, here received its apt embodiment, as the most dreaded power of evil. The Rabbins were never tired of recounting adventures in which Asmodeus and historical personages had played their parts, and the apocryphal book of Tobit presents an instance of one of these episodes. Asmodeus, however, is only bad in the main, without being wholly devoid of generous feelings : he could be moved by pity, and could even use his power for good purposes. He was a Persian demon, but not the Persian *god* of evil : he answered the Jewish conception during a transition period, when there were still hosts of good spirits engaged in perpetually ministering to humanity, and hosts of demons counteracting and thwarting these good offices : each spirit, good or bad, a personal being, and not a mere abstraction. Asmodeus was reigning at the period of which the Gospels treat, he was no doubt " the devil " who tempted Jesus in the wilderness, employing the lusts of appetite and power as his allies. The more philosophical Christian writers drew gradually away from the somewhat human Asmodeus, and abstracted the idea of evil until the arch-fiend's character became one of unmixed malignancy, consisting of nothing but evil, and incapable of any other motive or result. This is another Persian ideal, that of Ahriman, the Anra-mainyu of the Zend religion, the god of evil. In the Persian system a complete dualism existed :

Ormuzd, Ahura-mazdu, the supreme Good, created all that was good, and inspired every good thought and action; Ahriman, the supreme Evil, created everything that was bad in itself, and everything that could oppose the work of Ormuzd; he marred and frustrated all the good that Ormuzd had created, and systematically attacked every good thought and action, and endeavoured to turn it into evil. Ormuzd and Ahriman were of equal origin, and practically of equal power, and, although the latter was destined some day to be overcome by, and subjected to, the former, yet in the meantime he enjoyed an ample share of success.

These principles and beliefs were sufficiently received and recognized by the Jews, to be passed on by them into the Christian creed, which proved a congenial soil : we find the Fathers fully persuaded of the power and number of the demons, and also of the great and implacable malignancy of " the devil." Still, so long as there were a heavenly host of angels and saints between man and Jehovah, and to a great extent, by their multitudinous offices of good to man, veiling Jehovah from his sight, so long the prince of the devils was equally unnoticed in the assumed presence of the legion of demons who worked out the details of the diabolical schemes. It was left for the Reformation and its sternest votaries to sweep away the saints and angels, the demons and devils, leaving

face to face, the Deity, as the abstract personification
of good, and Satan, as the abstract personification of
evil, each pulling down the strongholds of the other,
and waging a perpetual warfare : by associating with
these ideas the doctrine of absolute predestination,
before the foundation of the world, for evil as well
as for good, the nearest possible approach to the
Persian dualism was made by some followers of
Calvin. It is often asserted, and strenuously maintained, that the Jewish and Christian doctrine has
never been that of the Persian dualism : that may be
true of the Jewish faith throughout, and of the early
and medieval Christians : but the seed of the Persian
dogma was sown in the Jewish mind during the
Captivity, was fostered and strengthened by after
intercourse, and although not appearing on the surface, it formed an under-current, hardly felt, but always present, until after the Reformation, when it
again reached the surface, and practically monopolized
the middle channel of the Christian creed; it had even
become more sombre, for instead of Ahriman being
destined to final reconciliation with Ormuzd, as the
Persians taught, we find Satan, and all his victims
and followers, doomed, without any sort of hope, to
everlasting fire, expressly prepared for them.

In the New Testament, Satan is either called by
his old Hebrew name of "Satanas," the adversary ; or
by that of " Diabolos," the Devil, the false accuser or

slanderer.[1] These two names are employed indiscriminately and interchangeably. In the account of the temptation in the wilderness, Matthew and Luke each call the tempter both Satan and the Devil; Mark only speaks of him as Satan.[2] In the parable of the tares and the wheat, the Devil sowed the tares;[3] and in that of the sower Satan snatched away the seed that fell by the wayside.[4] The identity is complete, and in the Apocalypse, Satan, the Devil, and the Dragon are expressly stated to be one and the same individual, a sort of Trinity of Evil.[5]

In the New Testament, Satan, the Devil, is undoubtedly a personal being and not a mere abstraction. He tempted Jesus in the wilderness; he tempts man to evil,[6] and was the direct agent inciting Judas to bring about the betrayal;[7] he works all kinds of evil, and resists all kinds of good, and is always on the watch for victims;[8] he is himself a transgressor of the divine law, and the father of all other transgres-

---

[1] The same word that is used as a name for the arch-fiend is used in St. Paul's injunction that deacons' wives and aged women should not be slanderers—i. e., "devils."—1 Tim. iii. 11; Titus ii. 3.

[2] Matt. iv. 1, 5, 8, 11—Devil; Ibid. 10—Satan; Luke iv. 2, 3, 5, 6, 13—Devil; Ibid. 8—Satan; Mark i. 13—Satan.

[3] Matt. xiii. 39.   [4] Mark. iv. 15.   [5] Rev. xii. 9; xx. 2.

[6] Acts v. 3; 1 Cor. vii. 5; 2 Tim. ii. 26.

[7] Luke xxii. 3; John xiii. 2, 27.

[8] Luke xxii. 31; Acts x. 38; 2 Cor. ii. 11; 1 Thes. ii. 18; 2 Thes. ii. 9.

sors ;[1] he assimilates the minds of men to his own
nature, and possesses and afflicts their bodies with his
own evil spirit ;[2] he can boast of his own synagogue ;[3] he
assumes the appearance of an angel of light ;[4] his
schemes are deep,[5] but he sits in high places ;[6] in
imitation of his divine enemy, he has his angels,
or messengers,[7] makes converts ;[8] and is politic, for
he does not mar his own work.[9] This formidable
adversary must never be out of mind, or yielded to,[10]
but must be resisted, and is indeed the typical enemy
to be cast behind the back.[11]

Michael, the archangel, contended with him,[12] and
he fell as lightning from heaven ;[13] he had the power
of death, but is now overcome ;[14] although under condemnation,[15] he is at large,[16] and even has opponents
delivered over to him for chastisement.[17] It is however the fervent hope of the Christian that he shall be
speedily bruised under foot,[18] and it is an article of
faith that he will be finally and everlastingly punished

---

[1] John viii. 44 ; Acts xiii. 10 ;
  1 John iii. 8.
[2] Luke viii. 12 ; xiii. 16.
[3] Rev. ii. 9 ; iii. 9.
[4] 2 Cor. xi. 14.
[5] Rev. ii. 24.
[6] Rev. ii. 13.
[7] 2 Cor. xii. 7.
[8] 1 Tim. v. 15.
[9] Matt. xii. 26 ; Mark iii. 23,
  26 ; Luke xi. 18.
[10] Eph. iv. 27 ; vi. 11 ; 1 Peter
  v. 8 ; James iv. 7.
[11] Matt. xvi. 23 ; Mark viii. 33.
[12] Jude 9.
[13] Luke x. 18.
[14] Hebrews ii. 14.
[15] 1 Tim. iii. 6.
[16] Rev. xx 7.
[17] 1 Cor. v. 5 ; 1 Tim. i. 20.
[18] Rom. xvi. 20.

in a lake of fire and brimstone,[1] expressly prepared for him and his angels.[2]

According to the orthodox Christian belief of the present day, Satan, the great spirit of evil, is the "enemy" of the human race, having originally fallen from heaven, and become the first introducer of moral and physical evil into the world, when, in the form of a serpent, he successfully tempted Eve : thenceforward he has been at enmity with the seed of the woman, causing all the diseases of mind and body from which man suffers, the tempter to all moral evil, and the prime instigator of every crime which has ever been committed. He is credited with most seductive powers, and an immense success in his schemes : the many travel on the broad road which leads to his realm, Destruction ; and the few escape by the narrow way that leads to Life. This work of destruction began with the first man who lived on the earth, and will continue until the earth itself shall pass away : and although he is destined to condign and everlasting punishment in Hell, he will have dragged down to the same Hell and punishment the vast majority of mankind.

In the meantime, Satan is endued with powers almost amounting to omniscience, omnipresence and omnipotence : he can read man's inmost thoughts,

---

[1] Rev. xx. 10.　　　　[2] Matt. xxv. 41.

and knows every detail of his life; he is always present to minister evil by temptation, to every human creature at the same time; and, with man's own carnal nature for ally, he is able to hurry millions to perdition, whilst only a few brands are plucked from the burning, and are "scarcely saved" from his power. He is the "god of this world," commanding the obedience of the whole hierarchy of evil spirits, "principalities, powers, rulers of the darkness of this world, and spiritual powers in heavenly places,"[1] and the King of Death and Hell.

This is Satan, the orthodox Devil of the Christian.

---

[1] Eph. vi. 12.

IV.

DEMONS.

In treating of demons, it is necessary to premise that there is a clear and well-defined distinction between a demon and a devil. They are both spiritual beings, but their attributes are essentially different. Originally, there were good as well as evil demons, although, in course of time, the term "demons" became exclusively identified with the idea of malignancy. Even then, however, their baneful influences were, in principle, not the result of a desire to injure, but simply of the fulfilment of their natural vocation ; causing injury, it is true, but injury which was not the object aimed at, and which might at times be mixed with good. The evils, on the contrary, ascribed to the Devil had their sole origin and motive in pure malignity—

Evil, be thou my good.[1]

The natural history of demons has received much and careful attention, and in result a tolerably clear idea of their nature and origin has been arrived at.

At the time that the history of the human race began, that is, when it first emerged from the period when neither written records nor continuous traditions were handed on from generation to generation ; the human inhabitants of the world who first created history, appear to have all belonged to the great Turanian race, of which the Chinese are still considered to be, in an especial degree, the representatives:[2] and to which the aborigines of America can with certainty be referred.[3]

It seems to be now satisfactorily established, that, at the dawn of history, these Turanian races extended over the whole habitable world ; and although they have to a great extent succumbed to other races, whose religions have superseded theirs, they have nevertheless left on the surface of the great sea of human belief the wreckage of their own dogmas, with which succeed-

---

[1] Milton, " Paradise Lost," B. 4. 110.
[2] Max Müller, " Science of Religion," 154, &c.
[3] Dawson, " Fossil Men," 203

ing religions have constructed a great part of their
own systems of faith.   Probably not a single race or
religion now exists which does not show distinct
signs of its Turanian inheritance, although that inheritance may be recognized as the most superstitious
part of its creed.   The Chinese and the American
Indians have preserved down to a recent period much
of their primeval Turanian character, and in a striking degree, their primeval theory as to demons.   The
main feature of the Turanian creed was, that the
whole of the Universe was peopled by innumerable
spirits; that every man, woman, and child had at
least two of such spirits ; that the sun, the moon, the
planets, and the stars, each had its demon; that
mountains, rivers, fountains, trees, clouds, winds, rain,
heat, cold, each had its demon; that many of these
had many demons each; that when the sun shone
beneficently, this effect was produced by its good
demon; when it parched up the land, producing
drought and famine, it was the act of the sun's evil
demon : that when it thundered and lightened, a war
of the demons of the elements was going on.   There
were also demons of the day, and demons of the
night; each fever and disease had its demon;
famine, drought, and every other scourge which
visits suffering humanity, had its special presiding
demon.   Indeed, it may be said, that to every object,
living or inanimate, of sufficient individuality to

receive a name, and to every abstraction which did receive a name, at the same time was attributed its demon. All these demons were of a permanent nature, and were assumed to have come into existence at the same time as the body or conception to which they were attached, and to have a commensurate duration; but besides all these, the world of demons was being perpetually recruited by human deaths, for it was a universal belief that the disembodied human soul became a demon as it separated from the body. Demons of this class have had attached to them characteristics as widely different as light is from darkness; but the true and original idea in the Turanian mind seems to have been, that disembodied souls were capable, under certain conditions, of becoming not only most powerful and exacting, but most malignant, if not satisfied in their own particular way. Hence the necessity for propitiating ancestral demons, and the introduction of the whole system of manes-worship, passing into sacrifices to the infernal powers for the dead, and masses for the repose of the soul. As Nature was most prolific and versatile in the production of forces out of which man created demons, so the fertile imagination of the human race has given to these demons a development, the ramifications of which could hardly be conceived, were the origin and history of that development not followed out and demonstrated. As

D

the demons of the cosmic forces were identified with might, strength and magnitude, they in time passed into the stage of penates, giants, solar and other heroes; the demons of the trees, rivers, fountains and seas, passed into dryads, nymphs, syrens and mermaids; ancestral spirits assumed the form of lares, familiar spirits, guardian angels and patron saints; whilst in certain morbid forms they were hobgoblins, ghosts, brownies and bogies; the forests and fields, the waves and caves, teemed with satyrs, fauns, fairies, elves, trolls and dwarfs. Thus it came about that the people of the ancient classical periods, of the middle ages, and even of quite recent times, could well believe that, were their eyes open, like those of Elisha's companions of old, they would see the world, and every corner in it, the earth, the air, the heavens, the seas, and the abyss, peopled with legions of spiritual beings, each with his office and vocation, and his separate, personal and intelligent existence; and all influencing, in some form or another, the affairs of the human race, in every minute particular.

> Millions of spiritual creatures walk the earth
> Unseen, both when we wake and when we sleep.[1]

We have hitherto been speaking of demons properly so called, as being spiritual beings immediately

---

[1] MILTON, *Paradise Lost*, b. 4.

DEMONS

representing a material substance, or a material conception; spirits that might be called "spirits appurtenant:" but besides these there were independent, unattached spirits, such as angels. It is difficult to define the point at which the host of angels became distinguishable from the good demons, who in their turn imperceptibly gradate into the doubtful and even malignant demons. Originally there was only one great system of spirits, out of which gradually but methodically the two classes of good and evil spirits were evolved. The first step towards the "differentiation" would naturally be to classify spirits in harmony with their material representatives; to attribute a powerful spirit to the sun, a destructive spirit to the tornado, a benignant spirit to the fertilizing dew, a ruthless spirit to the plague, and so on through the world of nature. The next step would be to subordinate spirits to one another, in the same relation as apparent in the material world; the sun disperses the clouds, the plague strikes down the man, therefore the spirit of the sun is more powerful than the spirit of the clouds, the spirit of the plague than that of the man. The spiritual world thus became disposed in a complete hierarchy, ranging from the supreme deities to the most insignificant fetish. The Talmudists maintained that the hosts of angels were 1,064,340,000,000,000 in number, and that the devils numbered 7,405,926, and that all these were divided into ranks and classes, "Thrones, dominations, virtues, princedoms, powers."[1]   "Abba Benyamin says : ' Were the eye permitted to see the malignant spirits, no creature could abide on account of them.' Abaii said, ' They are more numerous than we are, and they stand about us as the earth of the trenches surrounds the garden beds.' Rav Huna said : ' Every one of us has 1,000 on his left side and 10,000 on his right.'"[2]   To this day, the devout Turk, at the conclusion of his prayers, bows to the right and to the left, as saluting the genii of good and evil respectively by whom he is attended.[3]

Thus, then, the belief in demons having been from time immemorial an integral part of the popular belief, it has contributed very largely to the notions entertained down to the present time of the devil himself.   Two references will suffice to show this connection.   Pan, one of the classical rural deities, closely associated with the satyrs and the fauns, is described as horned and goat-footed, with a wrinkled face and a flat nose.[4]   Although this latter organ is often modified in its form, yet there is little difficulty in recognizing the horned and hoofed devil of popular tradition and nursery dread.   Again, Puck is a fair

---

[1] Farrar's "Life of Christ," ii. 466.
[2] Hershon's "Pentateuch according to the Talmud," 299.
[3] Lenormant's "Chaldean Magic," 144.
[4] Keightley's "Classical Mythology."

specimen of the Scandinavian dwarf or elf, the frolicsome embodiment of mischief:—

> I'll lead you about a round,
>   Through bog, through bush, through brake, through brier;
> Sometime a horse I'll be, sometime a hound,
>   A hog, a headless bear, sometimes a fire,
> And neigh, and bark, and grunt, and roar, and burn,
> Like horse, hound, hog, bear, fire, at every turn.[1]

We have here a mischievous demon, who, if seen at work carrying out his threats, would certainly be dubbed "the Devil."

A few words as to the process by which the aboriginal mind came to believe in the existence of spiritual beings. At first sight it may appear incomprehensible that man in a primitive state, barely emerging from the condition of the brute, should conceive such an abstract idea as that of a spiritual power, invisible, intangible, and in fact out of the reach of any of the senses. The savage's uneducated mind could probably not have bridged over so wide a chasm as that between the physical and the ideal, but for certain stepping stones which half suggested the conclusion. The associated ideas of cause and effect, which lie at the foundation of all intelligence, are however sufficient to account for the belief in spiritual beings; and that belief, once entertained,

---

[1] "Midsummer Night's Dream," act iii, scene i.

the door is open by which the infinite ramifications of
the idea can troop in.

Man in his early intellectual infancy began " to
take notice," seeing certain effects, and wondering
about the cause ; he saw that every solid body, living
or dead, had two fugitive attendants, a shadow and
a reflection, the former dark and dull, the latter
much more bright and lively.   The optical cause of
these appearances was not recognized, and the nervous
fear always attendant upon ignorance, gave to each
its individuality, calling the one a shade, the other a
soul, or psyche.   Experience taught that the shade
and psyche were directly connected with and dependent upon the body, but in a somewhat different
relation to it ; a man died, and you no longer saw
his shadow ; but, in the visions of the night, the well-
known figure of the dead man as he had appeared
in life, with his panoply and bearing, his voice and
mien, flitted past the dreamer ; hunting and fighting,
commanding and threatening, as in the days gone by :
the figure, not that of the dull dark shade, but of
the lively, fitful psyche, as seen in the water, or
reflected in the polished mirror-surface.   The man
in life had had body, shade and psyche : the dead
man's body was known to be mouldering in the
grave, the dreamer's body inert in sleep—death's
counterpart ;—but the psyches of the dead man and
the dreamer were holding intercourse together, much

as they had been wont to do when both in the body ;
and the inference seemed irresistible, plain to demonstration, that the dead man and the living dreamer
each had a something, more ethereal than the body,
which lived in spite of the body's death, visiting one
at the dead of night, continuing apparently the
business and occupation of former days, and interesting itself in the affairs of the survivors; com-
municating with them through their psyches, when
their bodies lay powerless in the similitude of death.
The vision was not that of the shade but of the psyche,
the body was gone and so was the shade; the body
was in the grave, the shade had been absorbed in the
darkness and gloom which imagination identified
with the tomb.

The apparition of the dead ancestor was by no
means shadowy and unpractical ; he may have been
a tyrant, or at least a stern imperious parent; and
when he returned in the visions of the night, he
brought back much of his old authority and influence,
deepened by the glamour involved in the very
weirdness of the apparition. With all the light and
knowledge which an advanced intellectual training
has given us in modern days, there are few of us who
could dismiss readily from the mind a dream in which
a dead parent seemed to stand before us, and, with
the familiar voice and gesture, unfold some secret, or
predict some momentous event : whilst in the dream,

the judgment and the will lie dormant, and the feelings and affections are open and unguarded ; but with us, when the light of day returns, our reason soon enables us to sweep away the fancies of the night : those, however, whose reasoning powers are low, or who have no certain knowledge to guide them, to whom dreams are undoubted facts, unaccounted for by waking thought and experience, see omens and portents in the dream episodes, and in the actors in them etherealized human beings. This becomes an earnest and honest belief, which grows into a firm faith, passed on from generation to generation : a man believes he has a spirit which will continue in a shadowy world the existence which in bodily life was experienced, and as he has seen his father's spirit after death busied in a round of occupations, with all the recognized adjuncts and circumstances, so he expects to be himself in like condition after death. He therefore enjoins upon his children as a filial duty to provide his disembodied spirit with all the neces· saries and luxuries which disembodied spirits rejoice in : and we may be sure that, if the children do not carry out the commands left by their parent, their conscience-stricken imaginations make the night hideous with dream visions of the offended ancestor, who will only be laid by compliance with his neglected commands, and the ease of conscience which duty performed induces.

The condition of the spirit's existence after death has been the subject of as much controversy and difference of opinion as it is possible to imagine. The opinions have differed according to the tastes and occupations of those who have formed them. The savage and the barbarian have always lived, and still live, in the element of the belief in spirits; but from the earliest time, even the most civilized and refined races have been thoroughly imbued with the same idea: " A belief in the persistence of life after death, may be discovered in every part of the world, in every age, and among men representing every degree and variety of culture."[1] Amongst cultured races the ancient Egyptians recognized after death a disembodied personality for each individual. The "Book of the Dead" proceeds throughout on this assumption; the soul has a form, and can eat and drink, while the man's shadow is part of his personality, and something substantial; it is taken from him at death, but restored to him in the second life.[2] The modern Basutos think that if a man walks on the river bank, a crocodile may seize his shadow in the water and draw him in.[3] The old cultured Egyptians and the modern savage Basuto agree pretty closely in theory.

---

[1] Renouf, " Hibb. Lec." 1879, 124.   [2] *Ib.* 153.

[3] Casalis Basutos, 245.

As a general rule, amongst all races, the spiritual state was merely a continuation of the earthly life, and whatever the idea of earthly happiness was, it was hoped that the spiritual life would be; and the dutiful family would provide, according to their power and judgment, for the contentment and well-being of the departed spirit.   The deceased was a hunter, and a warrior; his horse, his dogs, his servants, and even his wives, were slain at his grave, that he might have horse, dogs, servants, and wives to supply his wants in the land of spirits; his arms and armour were buried with him, that he might have their use : and so with money, clothes, and every other article of use or luxury.   In that spirit-land " the soul of the dead Karen, with the souls of his axe and cleaver, builds his house and cuts his rice; the shade of the Algonquin hunter hunts souls of beaver and elk ; walking on the souls of his snow-shoes, over the soul of the snow."[1]   The axe and cleaver, and the snow shoes, were accordingly dedicated to the dead, and buried with them.

It is not necessary here to examine more minutely the ideas entertained by savage, barbaric and civilized races as to the nature of the spirit, or soul, and its relation to the body; this has been done most ably and exhaustively by Mr. Tylor in the chapters on

---

[1] Tylor's " Prim. Culture," ii. 75, second ed.

Animism in his "Primitive Culture:"[1] it is sufficient for the present purpose to point out that, from the earliest dawn of intelligence, the belief in the existence of ancestral spirits has been almost universal, and still exists in the large majority of creeds.

The aboriginal human inhabitants of the earth, and especially the Turanian races, may be safely credited with the origination of the worship of ancestral spirits or manes. The American Indian tribes, of all stages of intelligence, address prayers to the spirits of their ancestors for good weather and luck in hunting : the Tasmanians bring their sick for healing to the funeral pile of a dead man : the Maoris of New Zealand believe that their deceased ancestors plead with the higher deities for the welfare of the living members of their families : the Vazimba, an aboriginal tribe of Madagascar, pay special attention to the tombs of their ancestors, which are constructed expressly with a view to offerings to the dead ; and the more modern races of the Malagasy have imbibed and continue the same doctrines and practices. Africa is a great stronghold of manes-worship : the Zulus rely upon their dead ancestors for success in battle, and they will speak of their father's spirit as present with them in daily life, and furthering the well-being of the family : in Southern

---

[1] London: Murray, 1873.

Guinea, not only offerings of food and drink are made to the deceased ancestor's spirit, but also a share of the survivor's profits in trade. In Asia the prevalence of manes-worship is still more remarkable: the Turanian tribes of Siberia, the Nagas and other aboriginal tribes of India, the Veddas of Ceylon, the Andaman Islanders, the followers of the Sin-tu faith in Japan, the lower orders of the Siamese, and in fact almost every race of men, firmly believe in the existence and sympathy of their ancestors' spirits, and reciprocate that sympathy in a hundred ways, living in the most constant and friendly relations with them. But it is amongst the 300 millions of Chinese, whose civilization is undoubtedly the oldest now in existence in the world, that manes-worship has attained its greatest perfection. They not only take their ancestors into confidence with regard to the daily occurrences of life, and seek and, as they think, obtain their powerful help (for by reason of their spirits being disembodied, their powers have become indefinitely increased), but they labour to glorify them, and by raising themselves in the social scale, believe that they are securing promotion in the world of spirits to their dead ancestors. It can thus be understood how greatly important it is considered that every man should leave surviving him a son by blood or adoption, to keep up the offerings and worship in which the ancestors stood in need : an idea which in varied forms reappears in the notions, and indeed in the laws, of many other races. China is like a great stratum of aboriginal ideas, standing out like a high table-land above the mass of newer races, which surging around has overflowed the older element in most other parts; there are nevertheless spots all over the world, where the same stratum crops out, although in a fragmentary form, and in a more or less modified degree the same principles are recognizable; such are the Vazimba, isolated in the mountains of Madagascar; the Veddas in the interior of Ceylon; and many of the other tribes to which reference has been already made. The Chinese race, out of their vast numbers, have developed a high state of civilization, and the isolated tribes, hunted, oppressed, and nearly exterminated by alien and strange races, have remained in the low condition in which they started, or may well have fallen lower, but the principle of ancestor-worship, common to them all, has survived this great divergence.

It may therefore be concluded that the low-class aboriginal tribes created the first idea of manes-worship, and having done so their idea turned out to be more robust than their race. In many instances, where the race has been completely stamped out or absorbed beyond all recognition, their religion and superstition have survived and been adopted by the conquering race. The Etruscan, and other kindred tribes, were no doubt of these absorbed races; and we therefore find the Romans, who absorbed them, maintaining the worship of the manes in full force; raising them to the rank of divine beings (Dii manes), erecting images and offering sacrifices to them, and relying confidently upon them for countenance and succour. The Greeks had similar rites, which are traceable to a like source. A practical illustration of the effect upon the Greek mind, produced by this belief in the necessity for manes-worship, is seen in the course taken by Leonidas in selecting the 300 warriors of Thermopylæ, who were expressly chosen because they "were all fathers with sons living." If they fell in their desperate encounter, their sons were left behind to perform the rites due to their fathers, and to the other ancestors of the family; and by belonging to a continued race, provision had been made for an indefinite performance of these kindly offices. On this principle celibacy was regarded by the Greeks as un- lawful; it was prohibited by Solon; and in Athens and Sparta it was treated even as a crime :[1] indeed, it is said, that "no man who knows he must die, can have so little regard for himself as to leave his family without descendants;" for then there would be no one to render him the worship due to the dead.[2] The same idea runs through the religious sentiment of

---

[1] Renouf, "Hibb. Lec." 143.   [2] *Ib.* 142.

other systematic religions : without a son to perform
the funeral rites, a Brahman believes that he cannot
enter into heaven :[1] and amongst the ancient
Egyptians, the " Ritual of the Dead," extending over
166 chapters, constitutes a most elaborate system of
rites, to be performed by survivors on behalf of a deceased, so as to ensure his safe passage over the waters
of the infernal Nile, thence through the Hall of Judgment, and the ordeal of the forty-two infernal judges,
into Aalu the Egyptian heaven, or Elysian fields.
The survivors would identify themselves with the
deceased, and, in his name, go through the ritual in
presence of his mummy, and continue this until all
danger was considered to be over : the evident belief
was, that the disembodied spirit, on its journey, was
accompanied by the ghostly counterpart of the
prayers and invocations which were taking sensible
form in the presence of the material body. The
deceased would thus, by proxy, vehemently maintain
his personal identity with Osiris, and his right to be
so considered, until the soul had passed all dangers,
and was declared to be absorbed into the essence of
Osiris himself, from whom he was originally but an
emanation.[2] Amongst the books on the mysteries of
the Babylonian religion, there was also a book en-

---

[1] Max Müller, "Hibb. Lec." 1878.
[2] Wilkinson's "Egypt," iii. 427.

titled "The Book of Going to Hades," which was probably similar to the Egyptian "Ritual of the Dead,"[1] although as yet no part of the work itself beyond its title has been recovered. The passing bell is still rung in many countries, to drive away the fiendish enemies of a dying man's soul, and secure the prayers of the faithful for its safe passage from earth to Paradise. The assistance rendered by the living to the dead is no longer that of food and raiment, but that of rites and invocations, to procure the protection from hostile spirits or demons; but the principle is throughout the same.

From the beatified spirits of our ancestors, and worship offered to them, we pass insensibly to deified men and heroes, and saints of medieval and modern times. We have seen that the sympathy existing between the dead and the living was mutual in its nature, arising upon an exchange of benefits—the party in the flesh exerting himself to procure the safe arrival of the dead man's soul into the happy land of spirits, and the dead man's spirit using his etherealized and accentuated powers for the benefit of the pious survivors: it is true, not necessarily furthering moral ends and desires, but repaying services rendered by supernatural assistance; assistance which a good spirit would confer to further a

---

[1] " Trans. of Soc. of Bib. Arch.," iii. 433.

good end, but which a bad spirit would dispense to aid a malicious purpose. One man would appeal to his patron saint, to deliver him from peril of ship-wreck, or some imminent distress; another would pray to a demon, the spirit of his dead grandfather, to lend his aid in the consummation of some fell scheme against the innocent, or to defeat the ends of justice. And each would base his claim to help on the sacrifices made or to be made at the shrine of the being invoked; the one would hang a silver ship on the image of the patron saint; the other would place a pot of meal or honey in the tomb where the demon's bones lay buried. The lower orders of the Siamese believe in gods of a high and potent order, but they fear to address them, lest through ignorance they should blunder in the complex ritual; they prefer to pray to the " parak," a lower class of deities, among whom the souls of great men take their places at death.[1] The modern peasant of the Roman or Greek persuasion will run through a list of saints at the first appearance of danger, and pray their intercession with the deity for deliverance. Romulus was the patron deity of children, he had a temple at Rome, where sick children were presented for their cure: the Roman women now present their sickly children at the church of St. Theodorus, the

---

[1] Tylor's " Prim. Culture," ii. 118.

patron saint of children, built on the site of the former temple of Romulus.[1] Helios, the storm-giving god, who traversed the heavens in his chariot of fire, had a temple at Mycene: the worship of Helios declined, and the religion of the Bible took its place; a church was built on the temple's site, dedicated to Elias, the prophet of the chariot of fire, whose prayers brought up the cloud, and made the heavens black with storm; the holy man of the Christian succeeded the sun-god of the pagan; but the name of the locality scarcely needed change from Helios to Elias, and local sentiment remained the same.[2] The Cornish miner Perran, who discovered the art of smelting tin long before the Christian era, drifts into the St. Piran who was the patron saint of miners: and now the tinners' great holiday, the Thursday before Christmas, is still called Pieron's day.[3]

"Although full ancestor worship is not practised in modern Christendom, there remains even now within its limits a well-marked worship of the dead. A crowd of saints, who were once men and women, now form an order of inferior deities, active in the affairs of men, and receiving from them reverence and prayer—thus coming strictly under the definition of manes. This Christian culture of the dead,

---

[1] Tylor's "Prim. Cult." ii. 121.   [2] Conway, "Demonology," i. 98.
[3] Max Müller, "Chips," iii. 312.

belonging in principle to the older manes-worship, was adapted to answer another purpose in the course of religious transition in Europe. The local gods, the patron gods of particular ranks and crafts, the gods from whom men sought special help in special needs, were too near and dear to the inmost heart of pre-Christian Europe to be done away without substitution. It proved easier to replace them by saints who could undertake their particular professions, and even succeed them in their dwellings." [1]

"To sum up the whole history of manes-worship, it is plain that in our time the dead receive worship from far the larger half of mankind; and it may have been much the same ever since the remote periods of primitive culture, in which the religion of the manes probably took its rise." [2]

The world of spirits has thus been recruited by vast numbers of the souls of departed men, whose power for good or evil has been recognized as influencing the affairs of mankind. What the man was in life, so his spirit is assumed to be after death; and as the teachers of religious ethics, particularly amongst Christians, have, as a rule, condemned as wicked the lives of the majority of men, so their spirits have been ranked as evil demons : and although the word demon, used for a departed soul,

---

[1] Tylor's "Prim. Cult." ii. 120.   [2] *Ib.* 123.

did not originally carry with it an evil meaning, it has now long since come to be regarded in no other light.

But there is another class of demons, the origin of which is more obscure, and which cannot in any way be referred to the idea of departed souls. In the oldest mythologies of the world—not those of the savage races, but those where culture has raised the thought from individual souls to abstract spirits—it has been a widely received dogma, that prior to the creation of man on the earth, not only were other forms of men created and destroyed, but also races of spirits, good and evil, who have a separate state of existence, and are either propitious or detrimental to man.

According to Berosus, the tradition of the Babylonians was that, prior to the creation of man, several other races of beings were created of monstrous forms, amongst which we recognize centaurs and other monsters of Greek mythology: and that some of these were totally destroyed before man's advent on the earth.[1] Another Babylonian legend, of Accadian origin, confirms this theory, and goes on to relate fierce wars between the armies of good and evil.[2] Another similar legend recounts a revolt in heaven and the casting out of a host of re-

---

[1] " Origines d'Histoire," 506.   [2] " Records of the Past," xi. 109.

bellious spirits :[1] a legend echoed by St. Peter and
St. Jude in their epistles,[2] and taken up by Milton,
and made the central episode of his immortal epic.

Rabbinical traditions assert that malignant demons
were created at the end of the sixth day of Creation,
and that the Sabbath, overtaking the work of
Creation, and absolutely enjoining rest,[3] there was
not time to do more than create their spirits, and
they were left without bodies ; and that ever since
they have had to wander about seeking bodies to
inhabit, in order that they may enjoy the pleasures
of material life. And this would seem to be the Jewish
method of accounting for demoniacal possession,
and would also explain the earnest prayer of the
legion of devils, cast out of the demoniac of Gadara,
that they should be allowed to migrate into the
herd of swine, rather than be wholly disembodied,
and driven into the limbo of chaos. The demons
thus created are described as having wings, they
sweep from one end of the world to the other, they
know the future like ministering angels, they eat
and drink, they propagate their species, and die like
men : they also know the future, by listening in
heaven behind the veil in the celestial sanctuary.[4]

The Arabian legends have a very similar theory
of the origin of the jinns, who correspond in most

---

[1] "Records of the Past," vii. 123.   [2] 2 Pet. ii. 4 ; Jude 6.
[3] Hershon's "Talmud," 80.   [4] Hershon, 69.
Conway, "Demonology," ii. 94.

particulars with the demons of the rabbins. The jinns were created out of fire, and occupied the earth for several thousand years before Adam : they were perverse, and would not reform, although prophets were sent to reclaim them : they were eventually driven from the earth, and took refuge in the outlying islands of the sea. One of their number, named Azäzeel (afterwards called Iblees) had been carried off as a prisoner by the angels ; he grew up amongst them, and became their chief, but having refused, when commanded, to prostrate himself before Adam, he was degraded to the condition of a sheytân, and became the father of the sheytâns, or devils. The jinns are not immortal, but destined ultimately to die : they eat and drink and propagate their species : they live in communities, and are ruled over by princes : they can make themselves visible or invisible, and assume the forms of various animals, such as serpents, cats and dogs. There are good jinns and bad jinns. They frequent baths, wells, latrines, ovens, ruined houses, rivers, cross roads and market places. Finally, like the demons of the Rabbins, they ascend to heaven and learn the future by eavesdropping. But with all their power and knowledge, they are liable to be reduced to obedience by means of talismans or magic arts, and become obsequious servants until the spell is broken.[1]

---

[1] Keightley's " Fairy Mythology," 25–27.

According to the modern Persians, there was a creation of spiritual beings, good and bad—the peris of surpassing beauty, and the deevs of equal ugliness, who suffered the same fate as the good and evil jinns, in punishment for disobedience. The beauty of the peris, like that of the most lovely women, is beyond description ; and from time immemorial has formed a stock subject for poets to dilate upon when in their most transcendental mood.[1] The repulsive deformity of the deevs, with ugly shapes, long horns, staring eyes, shaggy hair, great fangs, ugly paws, and long tails, has been an equally fertile one for pictorial illustration and word-painting.[2] A perpetual war rages between the peris and the deevs : they are both mortal, although endued with prolonged life : they partake of the sentiments and passions of men, although much superior to them in power. Talismans and magic arts will aid men to subjugate these deevs, and counteract their malice.[3]

We may now pass to other latitudes and races ; but, with variations easily accounted for by differences of climate and other surroundings, the legends are much the same. Throughout the whole Gotho-German race, mythology and folk-lore teem with notices of alfs (or elves) and duergar (or dwarfs).

---

[1] Keightley's " Fairy Myth." 22.　　[2] *Ib.* 23.　　[3] *Ib.* 15–17.

The whole world is full of spirits. The white alfs are good and friendly towards men, dwelling in a city of their own (Alf-heim) whiter than the sun in appearance. The dark alfs, or duergar, are equally inimical to man : they inhabit the air, sea and earth. And, of the last, those inhabiting thick woods, desert and lonely places, rocks and hills, are most malignant and mostly to be feared. They are also said to dwell beneath in the ground, and to be blacker than pitch. The origin of the duergar is stated in the Edda to have been in the clay, like maggots in flesh. They are described as in the form of men, but of low stature, with long legs, and arms reaching almost down to the ground when they stand erect : they are marvellous metal workers, both for gods and men, who place inestimable value on their works in gold, silver, iron or other metals.[1]

It is a prevalent opinion in the North that all the various beings of the popular creed were once worsted in a conflict with superior powers, and condemned to remain till doomsday in certain assigned abodes ; the dwarfs in the hills ; the elves in the groves and leafy trees ; the hill people in caves and caverns ; the mermen, mermaids and necks, in seas, lakes and rivers ; and the river-men, in small waterfalls : but that in the end they will

---

[1] Keightley's " Fairy Myth." 63, *et seq.*

be saved as well as all mankind.[1] In many parts of
Germany, and in other countries too, the idea
prevails that the dwarfs and elves are fallen angels.

The elves of the popular creed are directly
descended from the dwarfs or duergar of northern
mythology; but at the date of Spenser's "Faëry
Queene" the elves had become amalgamated with
the older fairies of romance, and both have come
down to us in an intermingled form.[2]

The pedigree of the fairies of romance is that of an
idea evolved from obscure traditions based on facts.
The earliest legends connect the idea of sorcery and
witchcraft with beautiful women. Lilith, the rabbinic
first wife of Adam, was gifted with marvellous beauty,
especially in her hair, and used spells and magic
arts.[3] A double of Lilith is probably to be found in
Leila, a leading figure of Persian romance, of inexplicable fascination; of dark complexion, with long
black hair, beautiful only to her lovers, but driving
them to madness. The Babylonian epic of Izdhubar[4]
records his being withstood on the sea-coast by two
women, Siduri and Sabitu, whom we may strongly
suspect of being sorceresses. Kirke is at once an
enchantress and a nymph of rare beauty.[5] The sibyls
were gifted with such magic as compelled even the

---

[1] Keightley's "Fairy Myth." 147, 148. [2] Ib. 59.
[3] "Con. Dem." ii. 93-98.
[4] Smith's "Chaldean Genesis," by Sayce, 264. [5] "Odyssey," b. 10.

gods ; and one at least of them was of such beauty
originally as to have been wooed by Apollo. The
gorgons, originally connected with the sea, have the
magic power of turning all who look upon them to
stone ; they, too, had beautiful hair, which in the case
of Medusa captivated Neptune and procured its
metamorphosis into serpents. The sirens also were
female nymphs who, inhabiting cliffs near the sea,
bewitched passing mariners by the sweetness of their
voices, and allured them to their death. These find
their exact counterparts in the lorelei of the Rhine,
and the mermaidens of all the Northern seas, endued
with irresistible powers of sweet music, by which
they allure mortals to their ruin ; they sing in sweet
and plaintive tones, and comb their golden hair. In
passing it may be noted that St. Paul refers to long
hair as the glory of a woman,[1] that mystic power
resided in the hair of Samson, and that Mohammed
had long hair. In the Apocalyptic vision, a swarm
of monstrous beings are, on the sounding of the
fifth trumpet, described as rising out of the smoke
of the bottomless pit ; they are composite and
monstrous in shape, endued with special powers
to hurt man ; they are under command of the
arch-fiend Apollyon,[2] and they have *long hair*.
Sorceresses and witches of all time have had

---

[1] 1 Cor. xi. 15.   [2] Rev. ix. 8.

dishevelled hair when entering on their sombre rites and incantations, and the Dame du Lac—a fay of romance—had wonderful hair.

Closely connected with the nymphs, are the Fates and Parcæ of mythology, and their representatives. Hovering over even the greatest gods of antiquity was a power, veiled, vague, but undoubted : inflexible decrees ordained a destiny which not even Jove himself could bend : and so in other creeds. In the beautiful legend of the descent of Istar to Hades found on the Babylonian tablets, even in the presence of the Queen of Hades, some power is called forth to judgment which seems to override her great authority—" the spirits of earth, seated on a throne of gold."[1] Among the Egyptians, the "hathors" are fair and benevolent maidens, daughters of Rā, the Sun, who preside at the birth of children, and fix their destiny. The hathors, daughters of the day, became to the Greeks and Latins the parcæ or fates, starting, spinning and cutting the thread of life and human destiny ; evolved from a single goddess, Mara, who acknowledged the superiority of no other deity, not even of Jove himself. The Erinys and Furies are near akin to the Fates :—

Chorus. Who then is the pilot of necessity ?
Prometheus. The triform Fates and the remembering Furies.

---

[1] Smith's "Chaldean Genesis," 245.

> *Chorus.* Is Jupiter then less powerful than these?
> *Prometheus.* Most certainly, he cannot at any rate escape his doom.[1]

The Scandinavians had their Nornir—the Past, the Present and the Future—maidens who come to each child that is born, to shape its life, giving gifts of good or evil, and foretelling its future fortune.[2]

The nymphs of classical mythology constitute another link between the ideas of the ancient and the modern worlds. They were a kind of middle beings between gods and men, partaking of the nature of, and in sympathy with, both; beautiful, ever youthful, cheerful and happy; long lived but not immortal; usually remaining in their particular spheres, in secluded grottoes or peaceful valleys by the fountains or streams, on the hills or in the woods or caves, of which they were the residing spirits; occupied in spinning, weaving, bathing, singing or dancing, or attending other deities in their expeditions of sport or revelry.[3] The nymphs were divided into classes, according to their origin, or the physical features with which they were identified: a Greek or Roman would have taken it as a matter of course, if, as he wended his way down a secluded ravine or shady glade, a bevy of beauteous damsels, the nymphs of the valley or stream, the woods or trees,

---

[1] Æsch. "Prometheus."   [2] Keightley's "Fairy Myth." 64.
[3] Murray's "Handbook of Mythology," 152.

had flitted across his path, their voices ringing out
sweet songs and merry peals of laughter, tripping
gracefully to the measure of wild but tuneful music :
and at last fading from sight as the notes died out
leaving him alone with the murmuring waterfall or
stream, or the silent wood. The nymphs were as
much an article of faith, as ever the saints of
medieval times have been, and the love and sympathy they inspired arose from a similar cause ; if
they were semi-divine, they were also semi-human.
The great gods were generally far away on Olympus
and out of sight ; the nymphs were attached to things
material, which formed a sort of body, coëval with
their own existence. The hemadryad's life was identified with her tree ; she would implore the woodman
to spare it, for if the tree died or was cut down, she
perished with it : this induced a feeling of frailty and
uncertainty, which appealed to human sympathies.

It is to be remarked that nymphs were often the
nurses and protectors of the gods and heroes ; and
the ocean nymphs had a special mission to rear the
children of men.[1] Nymphs were mostly beneficent,
but not always so ; for one class at least—the
limnads, nymphs of lakes, marshes and swamps—
were dangerous beings, alluring and misleading travellers by their songs, or mimic screams for help.[2]

---

[1] Keightley's " Cla. Myth." 215.   [2] Murray's " Mythology," 154.

As Greek and Roman traditions waned in popu-
larity, and the romance of knight errantry followed
in the track of the barbarian inroads on the Roman
Empires, the Roman and Greek nymphs ceased to
be recognized as such, but their places were taken
by other beings, not less interesting, not less beautiful, but partaking of the weird attributes which
always characterized the faith of the invaders from
the wild and frowning North. The fays of romance
were beings of supernatural beauty and powers, able
to become invisible at will, and transport themselves
from place to place in a moment of time, often in
assumed forms, and by enchantments and spells to
subjugate humans to their will ; they were, moreover,
susceptible of human passions, and their intrigues
with ordinary mortals form the staple of medieval
romance. In these respects, the fays closely repeat
the history of the nymphs, and when their name is
traced to its origin the resemblance is as close as
ever. The term "fay" (French, *fée*) has been traced
to two derivatives, both worked out with consider-
able ingenuity and plausibility : they are probably
both founded in fact. The Latin word *fata* was
used for the parcæ or the fates, to whom reference
has been already made, and this word appears to
have passed into all the dialects of the romance
language in use in the Middle Ages, and to have
been then used to describe the beings whom we now

know as the fays of romance : *fata,* Italian ; *fada,*
Provençal ; *hada,* Spanish ; *fée,* French ; *fays,*
fairies, English. The other derivation is from Latin
fatare (derived from *fatum* or *fata*) to enchant ; this
passed into French as *faer* to enchant ; with the par-
ticiple *faé,* and we read of *chevaliers faés* and *dames
faées.* The modern expression to represent a fairy
has become *fée* in French, and *fay* in English ; their
domain, *faërie,* and, finally, the denizens of faërie,
fairies.[1]

As a characteristic example of the fays of romance,
may be mentioned a legend of the Dame du Lac, who
was a pupil of Merlin the enchanter, from whom she
learnt the art of magic, and who requited her instructor by entrapping him in a rock, and transport-
ing him as a prisoner to fairy-land. At another
time, King Ban was dying of grief caused by base
treachery : his queen, having placed her new-born
babe on the margin of a lake, was soothing the
monarch's last moments ; she returns to the lake and
finds the babe in the arms of a beautiful lady ; no
entreaties will prevail upon her to return it, and without a word she plunges into the lake with the child.
The lady was the Dame du Lac ; the lake itself was
but an illusion raised by enchantment : the babe was
trained by the fay, and became the Lancelot du Lac

---

[1] Keightley's "Fairy Myth." 5, &c.

of King Arthur's court.   We trace here some of the
mischief of the old lake nymphs, the limnads.

The fays of this period are not diminutive in size,
as we now conceive the fairies, but resemble ordinary mortals so much as to be mistaken for them,
and in fact to enter into matrimonial alliances and
intrigues with them.   The fays of romance were,
however, doomed to rapid degeneration.   Running
parallel with their history was that of another class
of beings, brought in by the northern hordes, who
had a folk-lore of their own, traced from a dim antiquity, and having an origin far removed from the
classic mythology of the south.   These were the
elves, the dwarfs or little people, themselves a race
of varied origin and varied attributes, and destined
to coalesce with the fays or fairies, and practically to
absorb them.   The accomplishment of this union is
best shown by the fact that, at the time of Shakespeare, Oberon is spoken of as the king of fairy-land,
and Titania as its queen.   Now Oberon is the same
as Elberich, the chief of the dwarfs, or elves of
German folk-lore,[1] and Titania is the same as Diana,[2]
the principal leader of the nymphs, who had since
been transformed into the fays.

The fairies of Shakespeare and our modern nurse-

---

[1] Keightley's " Fairy Myth." 208.
[2] Ovid, "Metamor." b. 3.   The poet records that the Goddess
was taller than all her Nymphs.

NYMPHS, DWARFS AND FAIRIES

ries require no description. We all know how they will come to a christening and fix the infant's destiny, not seldom mixed with a dash of spite. As man's faith in, and respect for, the supernatural influence has dwindled, so has the realization of the beings exercising it. Diana, the dreaded Artemis, granddaughter of the first and greatest of the Titans, and sprung from Jove himself, and who was also one of the twelve great Olympian deities, has dwindled down to Titania, the fairy queen, who despatches her subjects with the command—

> Some to kill cankers in the musk-rose buds;
> Some war with rear-mice for their leathern wings,
> To make my small elves coats.[1]

Whilst the fays and elves and all the varied streams of beings, which have contributed to their pedigrees, have now shrunk into one small common stream, fast drying up in the sands of thought, some of the conceptions from which they sprang, at an early date diverged and struck root independently. This new departure produced a most luxuriant growth, which has since become as important in the world's history as the other has faded into insignificance.

Starting from the general principle that everything in heaven and earth had its spirit, we can at

---

[1] "Midsummer Night's Dream," Act ii. sc. 3.

F

once understand how good things and beneficent phenomena had good and beneficent spirits. When the expanse of heaven was regarded as the most sublime object that could be presented to the senses, the great spirit of the heavens was looked upon as the Supreme God, the originator of all other spirits, and the creator of all things in heaven and earth— the Father in Heaven. The sun and moon, and the five other planets come next in the order of sublimity; far beyond the reach of man, moving about the heavens, of apparent set purpose, and not like the other stars; their spirits therefore came next in order in the heavenly hierarchy, and amongst the star-gazing people of Chaldea, imposed a veneration for the number seven, which has reverberated throughout the world, and is still instinct with life in our midst at the present day: we thus have amongst the Chaldeans seven gods of the seven planets, and among the ancient Persians or Zends, Ahura-Mazdu associated with the seven Amshaspands, immortal saints who assisted him in the government of the world. The Jews had their archangels, each one with a host of angels under his command: the Egyptians had good genii in the service of Osiris : and in the Apocalypse we read of the seven lamps before the throne of God, which have their seven angels, the watchers,—or unsleeping ones,—to whom was committed the care of the seven Christian Churches.

One star after another was seen to dart across the heavens; these were messengers sent on special missions of mercy or retribution. Or the falling star, apparently torn from its place and suddenly cast down into darkness, had its spirit, which in like manner was cast out of heaven; one of the wandering stars to whom is reserved the blackness of darkness for ever.[1]

The innumerable stars, the host of heaven, each one with its attributed spirit, most naturally furnished the Great Spirit and the archangels with messengers and attendants; and so we find them continually described both in sacred and secular literature. These angels are perfectly pure spirits, without sin and invisible; they are "messengers" and ministers of God's will and purposes, nothing is too great or too insignificant for them to perform; they will destroy Sodom with fire and brimstone, or tend the growth of a wayside herb. Their number is beyond computation, outnumbering the inhabitants of the world in the proportion of a million to one.[2] These hosts of angels passed on from the Jewish faith into the Christian creed: no wonder that in view of such a wealth of beneficent spirits, man should have concluded that one of their number was specially commissioned to guard and defend him

---

[1] Jude 13.   [2] Farrar's "Life of Christ," ii. 466.

from danger, and that each man, woman and child should have a guardian angel, or even more than one. The Chaldeans had each a guardian god and goddess living in him as his protectors : the ancient Persians, as well as all the stars, animals, and even angels themselves, had each his " Fravishi," who was invoked in prayers and sacrifices, and was the invisible protector who watched untiringly over the being to whom he was attached.[1] Each Jewish child had his guardian angel, who always beheld the face of his Father who was in Heaven.[2] And these guardian angels have passed on into Christian times, and have only yielded to the more material but perhaps more easily recognized saint, who, having done battle with human infirmities, is felt to be more accessible to the wants of a struggling mortal. The Latin "Genius" and the Egyptian "Ka," both variants of the same ideal, were spiritual beings which seem to have been on the border land between the individual soul and the individual's guardian spirit, and it is difficult now to determine which of these two characters they more resembled.

It will thus be seen that the belief in angels, and in guardian angels, brought down to the present day, and still widely held with all the sanctions of accepted religions, is but a branch from the same

---

[1] Lenormant's "Chaldean Magic," 199.   [2] Matt. xviii. 10.

root :—the existence of spirits associated with each material object or person,—which gave birth to the belief in nymphs, fairies, and elves, and all the other spiritual denizens of mythology and folk-lore.

Another branch of the world of spirits was developed into the great class of cosmical spirits, represented as being in some form or other the off-spring of the earth, as having made war upon the gods of Heaven, and having been conquered and thrust down to the lowest depths of Hell, to Tartaros, there to undergo punishment for their rebellion.

The Chaldeans had seven " ensnarers" whom they called " Maskim ;" demons dwelling in the bowels of the earth, and surpassing all others in power and in terror : these cause convulsions of the earth, disturb the motion of the stars,

> They violently attack the dwellings of man,
> They wither everything in the town or in the country.
> They oppress the free man and the slave.
> They pour down like a violent tempest in heaven and earth.[1]

These are the seven "rebellious spirits," powers of evil, which in the "days of storms," against high heaven plotted evil;[2] they are the dreaded enemies, against whom the highest and most potent gods are invoked with the reiterated wild cry :—

> They are seven, they are seven !
> Twice over they are seven![3]

---

[1] Lenormant's " Chaldean Magic," 29.
[2] "Records of the Past," v. 163.   [3] *Ib.* iii. 143.

These rebel spirits reappear amongst the Greeks as the Titans, the children of Titania, the earth; who, for the most part, are personifications of the wild, powerful, and obstructive forces of Nature. The Titans warred against Jove, the god of heaven, the earth crashed in conflagration, the forests crackled, the ocean boiled, and threw up scalding vapour to the sky, as thunderbolts and lightnings flew whirling down from heaven, the winds adding to the din and increasing the strife, until the sound was as of the earth falling in ruins, and of a solid heaven like a vast avalanche, dashing down upon it from above.[1]

The battle ended by the Titans being overcome, and driven headlong into Tartaros, a dark and dreary place where are the extremities of earth :—[2]

> The gaping gulf low to the centre lies,
> And twice as deep as earth is distant from the skies.
> The rivals of the gods, the Titan race,
> Here sing'd with lightning roll within th' unfathom'd space.[3]

Such too were the great frost giants of the Eddaïc mythology. A mass of frozen venom had originally produced the giant Ymir, out of whom was formed the earth, and who became the father of the frost giants. The destruction of these giants was brought about by Bör, the father of the gods of heaven, the Eddaïc Jove :—[4]

---

[1] Hesiod, 690.   [2] *Ib.*   [3] " Æneid," vi.
[4] Mallet's " Northern Antiquities," 402–405.

> Mountains together dash,
> Giants headlong rush,
> And Heaven in twain is rent.[1]

Finally we note that Job recognized that the Rephaim, "the mighty ones," were confined in the depths of Sheol, groaning and trembling at Jehovah :[2] that Isaiah identifies the Rephaim with the "other lords," whose name had been invoked as gods, but whom Jehovah had destroyed, and had made their memory to perish, turning them into "Rephaim"[3] and that the Apostle Peter quotes the angels that sinned, and whom Jehovah had cast down into Tartaros, and delivered them into chains of darkness, to be reserved unto judgment.[4]

It is not improbable that, through all these traditions, in which dread powers of terrific influence and mien are dimly seen, comes down to us the echo of a mighty and cruel religion, in which the powers of earth were deified, and their worship cruel, bloody and relentless, sensual and degrading ; when the only offering acceptable to the gods was human blood, and the standard of morality that of the Pans and Satyrs : when "the earth was corrupt and filled with violence."[5]

We have seen that the most dreaded cosmical spirits were considered as the offspring of the earth,

---

[1] Mallet's "Northern Antiquities," 402   [2] Job xxvi. 5.
[3] Is. xxvi. 13, 14.   [4] 2 Pet. ii. 4.   [5] Gen. vi. 11.

and in Northern Mythology the duergar, who were its earth spirits, whose abode was in the ground and in stones, were said to have been bred in the earth as maggots are in flesh.[1]   The duergar were a repulsive race of beings, of low stature, with short legs and long arms, reaching almost down to the ground when standing upright; gifted with much knowledge, and especially skilled as metal-workers.[2]   After the duergar became personified and familiar to the popular mind, their origin as cosmical spirits, in which they resembled the Titans, Rephaim, and other subterranean monsters, was gradually lost sight of; and they were classed with any race of actual men who combined in themselves a sufficient number of such attributes as, to the careless and ignorant, present some features of resemblance.   At this point come in the dwarfs.

The dwarfs or trolls are represented as dwelling inside hills, mounds, and hillocks; sometimes in single families, sometimes in societies.   They are regarded as extremely rich.   Their hill dwellings are very magnificent inside; and, on great occasions of festivity, are lighted up, and seem to be full of treasure, and sumptuous furniture and utensils. The dwarfs are obliging and neighbourly, keeping up friendly intercourse with mankind : equally sensitive

---

[1] "Prose Edda," 13.   [2] Keightley's "Fairy Mythology," 67.

to kindness and to slight, requiting the former with gratitude, and resenting the latter with manifest petulance. They marry, have children, and live much as mankind do :—even at times intermarrying with them. They are generally low in stature, hump-backed, with long crooked noses and twinkling mischievous eyes ; dressed in grey or brown jackets, and wearing red caps. They are much addicted to dancing, music and singing, in which they specially indulge at festival time. They have supernatural powers, which they exercise not only for their own benefit, but by which they influence the lives and destinies of mankind ; they can confer bodily strength and beauty, prosperity or mischance ; they can fore-tell future events, and spirit themselves or others away, either in an invisible state, or in the form of animals or other beings, and this by means of spells, talismans and charms.

Whilst possessing all these wonderful powers, they are themselves the slaves of magical influences, and at times become suddenly subdued and helpless by some chance accident. Usually invisible to mortal sight, they become suddenly visible if their cap gets knocked off and seized ; and until they regain it they are in the power of the possessor of the cap. In other ways they may at times be captured by mortals, and made to reveal and give up their treasures, or otherwise subserve the interests of their captor.

They are however a very slippery set, and although inferior in size are sometimes endued with great strength and agility, and always with a watchful cunning which makes them more than a match for the ponderous beings of a duller mould: the cap of invisibility will be suddenly snatched back and resumed, or the vigilance of the captor will be eluded just at the critical moment, and the dwarf will vanish with a ringing jeer.

All dwarfs are not however equally good-natured, some being more grim than others, and seeming to rejoice in malicious spite: but as a rule they are harmless, shy, and retiring, timid when not in large numbers, suspicious, and occasionally morose. They are not particularly honest, but their dishonesty consists more of pilfering than serious robbery, and only being of a serious character when women or children are carried off,—kidnapping being a particular weakness of theirs. Their mischief is also more of a petty than of a serious nature; skimming the milk, breaking the crockery, worrying the cattle, and such like: or misleading or scaring travellers or their horses, inveigling them into dilemmas or leaving them to flounder in swamps or quagmires.

They are often represented as metal workers of great and unrivalled skill;[1] being able to fashion work

---

[1] Keightley's "Fairy Mythology," 176.

of silver, gold, and steel of incredible fineness, strength and durability. Tradition is full of instances where gold and silver goblets, rings and chains, have been obtained from them, sometimes by fair means, and sometimes by foul : and their swords, armour, and coats of steel mail have a lightness, temper and strength which make their happy possessors at the same time irresistible and invulnerable. Even in such common-place items as ploughshares and other agricultural implements, their neighbours sought, and with proper consideration, obtained from them, their assistance, although the mode and plan of working were kept a profound secret, and were rarely intruded upon.

With all this occult knowledge and superiority in certain " arts and mysteries," the dwarfs were behind their human fellow-creatures in some of the more every-day subjects : naturally quick-witted, they were not readily receptive of new ideas of civilization. A tale is told of a company of Korreds, (Dwarfs of Brittany,) succeeding in counting up a sequence of days sufficiently to make up a chorus of—

> Monday, Tuesday, Wednesday ;
> Monday, Tuesday, Wednesday—

and getting no further until taught by the tailors Peric and Jean, to go on to " Thursday and Friday and Saturday and Sunday."[1]

---

[1] Keightley's " Fairy Mythology," 439.

Upon a full examination of the traditions and monuments of the earliest ages, it is impossible not to conclude that the dwarfs and trolls must be identified with primeval races of men of low stature; who covered a large area of the habitable globe, and who were gradually driven into mountain-fastnesses, swamps, ice-bound tracts, or trackless steppes, before the steady advance of a larger, more powerful, or better armed race of men. This fluctuation of races has undoubtedly taken place in most parts of the world : the invading element not always being the intrusion of the larger races on the smaller, but sometimes of the smaller on the larger. Hence we have traditions coming down from the smaller race, recording their own victories over the larger one; in which they speak of themselves as ordinary men of normal size, and their enemies as giants : and they boast of their own cunning, whereby they outwitted the clumsy and stupid giants, their ponderous strength notwithstanding. The nursery tale of Jack the Giant Killer is no doubt a tradition of this class. When on the other hand the history is recounted by the larger race they in their turn refer to themselves as ordinary men, and the enemy become a race of dwarfs or pigmies, whose treachery and cunning, nimble activity and unexpected resources, incomprehensible to the slower intellect of the narrator, invest them with attributes of supernatural powers. This not only engenders fear and superstition in relation to the little people when alive, but, when they are dead, haunts the places of sepulture—the caves and huts where they lived, and the dolmens and barrows where they were buried,—and creates an equal and indeed a much greater dread : for, be it remembered, every one without exception believed implicitly in the spirits of the dead being endued with accentuated powers, and haunting the localities where they had passed this life, and the places where their bodies were laid.

The Accadians, who were amongst the earliest, if not the earliest, inhabitants of Babylonia, were eminently gifted with all the culture of the ancient world ; they professed to be the heirs of an older extinct society,—the world before the Flood—and to have alone received the last words of the occult sciences which the perished races of man had built up through cycles of life and culture. One cannot help suspecting that the Accadians represented the nucleus of the original Turanian stock, which had from time to time thrown off the vast hordes of ever teeming races, which had spread throughout the world, and which eventually were elbowed out by the stronger and larger races of men. The Accadians themselves had to yield to the ferocious Assyrian conquerors, and to see political power pass from their hands for generations, until their conquerors were themselves subdued by the steady force of culture and superior intelligence

which the physically conquered race possessed. The
dread powers of magic, astrology, and other occult arts
restored to the Chaldeans the sway which had been
wrested from their Accadian ancestors. In the great
Indian peninsula successive hordes of Aryan invaders
from the North-Western mountains poured down into
the plains of Hindustan, and passed over to the island
of Ceylon : the lofty stature and the fine physique of
this handsome race was more than a match for the
aborigines of low Turanian type whom they found in
possession of the land : centuries of persistent
aggression have driven these races from the greater
part of the country, either overwhelming them or
absorbing and subjugating them : but still the Nagas
and Nautch people of the main-land hills, and the
Veddas of the interior of Ceylon remain to testify
by their very distinct physical characteristics, and
their social and religious customs and superstitions,
that they belong to the great Turanian stratum of the
human race, or were once incorporated with it. The
great continent of Northern Asia, the teeming millions
of China, and the wandering Tartar tribes, have in the
main resisted the inroads of intruders, and present,
some in a state of culture and others of barbarism,
probably the most perfect examples of the old Turanian nature. In Europe the Lapps, the Finns, the
Esthonians, the Etruscans, the Basques, the Iberians,
with other kindred races, once overspread the whole

continent and the British isles: the Celts, Gauls, and Scandinavians, and other Aryan races, surged over them in successive waves, to some extent absorbing as they went, but leaving a few isolated groups of the old people, sufficiently distinct for recognition, in the present day, amongst whom still survive in some vitality, traditions of the little cunning people of primeval times, or the physique and the social customs which characterized them. Such traditions are to be found amongst the Bretons and Basques, in the hills of Wales, Cornwall, Devonshire and Derbyshire, the Highlands of Scotland, and the outlying islands, and the wilder parts of Ireland; all places where the shattered remnants of a hounded race would linger longest until extinguished or absorbed into other races; and when indeed such races were absorbed, they would perpetuate a strong complexion of their own physical and mental character. The old physique and social customs are most to be remarked amongst the Lapps, who, a small and feeble race, have been driven into the outer circle of the habitable world, where existence is too miserable to be envied, and the country almost too inhospitable to be intruded upon. But here we have preserved an easily recognizable type of the old dwarf race, living either under ground or in conical beehive huts, and with the main features and traditions of their ancestors, modified only by the necessities of their position and mode of life.

In America the Eskimos, who certainly at one time overspread a far greater tract of the continent than they now do, have been like the Lapps shut out in the cold by the world's household, as the only condition upon which their continued existence would be tolerated. It is here to be remarked that probably in America the order of conquest was to some extent reversed, that at one time the primeval inhabitants were of a higher physical type than their conquerors, and that it was only in consequence of a long period of peace, prosperity, and plenty, that they became so effeminated as to be unable to withstand the inroads of the fierce but small Aztecs who were genuine representatives of the Turanian type. Dr. Dawson in his "Fossil Men," has argued, with much force, that the Alleghans were the oldest inhabitants of the North American continent of whom any trace can be found; that they were a mild, peaceable, prosperous, and effeminate race, living in large communistic dwellings capable of lodging as many as 600 families under one roof; and that they fell an easy prey to the blood-thirsty, cruel, and hardy Aztecs, who in point of stature were nevertheless a much smaller race of men.[1]

Now what are the characteristics of the Turanian race which fossil remains and recognizable history enable us to identify? They were all short, obese

---

[1] "Fossil Men," by Dawson, 51–66.

and swarthy; with dark hair, crisply curled, and scanty beards, high cheek-bones, and obliquely set dark eyes : these physical characteristics are seen in the portraits of ancient Etruscans and the Latin records of them,[1] and in the descriptions of the Scythians,— the roaming peoples of the whole Northern world. The remains of many of the neolithic men are in complete accordance with these features, and although we have not any precise information on the physique of the Accadians, yet other circumstances seem to combine to picture to us as probable a similarity to other Turanian races. In modern times the Tartar tribes of Asia, the Nagas, the Lapps and Eskimos, have a greater resemblance to those ancient races than any others now extant. Again, wherever the dwellings of primeval man are traced, if they do not consist of caves and holes in the earth, they generally are found to be in a beehive form and partly underground ; dwellings of this pattern are still used by the Lapps and Eskimos, and traces of prehistoric huts of this form are found very generally all over the world. Another form of dwelling which was largely adopted, was that of the communal dwellings before referred to as in use amongst the Alleghans : traces of this system are also found in Sweden, in Mexico, Yucatan, Peru and Africa, and probably the

[1] Taylor, " Etruscan Researches," 61.

Swiss lake dwellings may have been of the same nature; the Greenlanders' winter houses certainly arc of that class.[1] Dr. Dawson suggests that the tradition of the Tower of Babel built on the Chaldean plain, refers to the construction of a huge communistic building on this plan, intended to bind together the early tribes of men in one vast communistic league.[2]

Before quitting this subject, reference should be made to the inhabitants of the Andaman Islands, who have recently been most carefully studied and ably described by Mr. E. H. Man. These interesting people would seem to be a pure and unmixed survival of the old Turanian races, and it would appear that their insular position and insignificance have saved them from destruction and contamination. Varied influences have been at work in almost every other part of the world, which have leavened and modified all its other inhabitants, to a greater or less extent : but in the case of the Andamanese we feel that we are in the presence of a race of men belonging to another and distinct creation, so great is the divergence from the ordinary types. The average stature of the men is 4ft. 10¾ inches and of the women 4ft. 7½ inches, and the average weight 98½ lbs. and 93¼ lbs. respectively. They are thick-set,

[1] Dawson, "Fossil Men." 83.   [2] Ib. 84.

sturdy, and active, but very short lived, dying generally at the age of about 22: they are simple-minded
and child-like, wanting many of the most common
rudiments of culture, not knowing how to produce
fire and not having in their language the means of
counting beyond two : their huts are of various
shapes, but large common dwellings are found amongst
them, and some of the beehive pattern : they have
very acute perceptions, being able to spear turtle in
the pitch dark night, guided in their aim by the
acute hearing which they possess, and distinguishing
among the jungle, animals and birds which to the
ordinary eye are not perceptible. They are most
industrious dancers and singers ; every event of life,
every transaction of business or pleasure leads to con-
certed dancing and singing, without which their life
would evidently come to a standstill. Their intellect
is by no means of a low order, for if taken in hand when
quite young their children will acquire rapidly a full
average of education ; a child of 13 has been known to
speak in four languages. Their character is described
as " merry, talkative, petulant, inquisitive, and rest-
less ; their speech is rapid, with a constant repetition
of the same idea : a joke, if it does not take too
practical a form, is heartily appreciated while all
insults or injuries are promptly resented." [1]

---

[1] *Journal of Anth. Inst.* xi. 285.

It is hardly necessary to point out that the Andamanese have so many points of similarity to the traditional description of the dwarfs, that it is fair to infer that they are identical in origin, and that the dwarfs of popular mythology and folk-lore are none other than Turanians of an early age, or at all events their ghosts or spirits, in which their main features and characteristics survive.

The vast number of the old Turanian tribes, the varied circumstances of their existence, the exigencies and influence of climate, caused great diversity in their state of culture ; and many groups of such tribes were remarkable for arts which others had not acquired. Thus the neolithic races made their weapons of flint, and dwindled away under the oppression of their bronze and iron-using invaders, leaving but little trace of their existence, beyond the vast numbers of their flint arrow-heads and other stone implements, and the confirmatory evidence of their identity with the dwarfs or elves, afforded by these arrow-heads being known as "elfin bolts" of magic power. But there certainly appear to have been other races of Turanians who acquired and exercised great skill in metal working, and thereby originated the legends of metal working dwarfs and trolls, which undoubtedly abound in the folk-lore of Europe.

Recapitulation.

We have endeavoured to trace how, from the observation of shadows, reflections and dreams, the human mind first conceived the idea of spirits; how this idea, in the first instance, attached itself to deceased ancestors, and from thence developed into manes-worship, the deification of heroes, and the canonization of saints: how the unexplained phenomena of nature led to the belief in nature spirits, generated independently of men, and therefore of another and perhaps prior creation; how the world became peopled with jinns, genii, demons and fravishis: how, parallel with these, the conception of inexorable fate or destiny beyond the range even of thought, came in as a controlling power, and that all other, even the highest, spiritual powers were bound by sorcery and magic forms: how this overruling power of fate and sorcery spread amongst the dread votaries of occult art, the sybils, fates, and nymphs; but softened away its terrors, as nymphs assumed a lovely human form, and entered into human intercourse: how, by degrees, the nymphs and fates of old melted into the fays and fairies of romance: how the northern invaders of Europe had inherited another form of nature worship, coloured by the grimness of their country and climate, and had realized their ideal in monstrous duergar and dwarfs : how these beings of the mind had received amplification by association with the dwarfs of actual life, the low type of aborigines, dwarf and uncouth, but cunning and wielding magical knowledge and power : how the duergar and dwarfs dwindled into elves, whilst the fays and fairies faded in like manner as they each passed down from power to pettiness and pranks, until eventually the two peoples made common cause and occupied fairy-land together ; Oberon, the dwarf, being their king, and Titania, the quondam nymph, their queen : how the great cosmical powers, who refused to sacrifice their greatness, and dwindle into toy spirits, were cast down from heaven, and as Titans, Rephaim, and fallen angels, chained and groaning in the depths below, serve to point the moral that opposition to the powers that be, is evil.

We have seen that all these beings are or have been classed as both good and evil in their time, that there are good demons and bad demons, good jinns and bad jinns, good genii and bad genii, kind fairies and spiteful fairies, propitious as well as fatal nymphs; that the Titans suffer only from the wickedness of having opposed those who were strong enough to overcome them, and that, even now, there are hosts of heavenly and infernal angels, who own a common origin and the divergence of whose career is not easily explained.

The intermingling of all these beings and the ideas of which they are the offspring is the result of ignorance, of limited knowledge and experience:—the Northern peasant has his runes of trolls and elves, his Roman neighbour has legends of nymphs and fays : they both find tombs and other traces of a dwarfish and strange race of men, and local records and traditions; all these have points of contact, and, floating on the uncertain sea of imagination from which they sprang, without any firm anchorage or attachment of fact, they drift together down the stream of time, and finish as a poetical conglomerate. This process is discernible in all subjects of tradition : the evolution is worked out by the decay of each component part, and the conglomeration of the degenerated residuum : as time obliterates a part of each tradition, it adds new matter from another source; and it is only by tracing each step of the process (often an impossibility) that the true source of each constituent part can be detected.

The English popular ideas of the Devil are very intimately connected with those about house spirits, hobgoblins, dwarfs, puck and pixies ; who were always conceived to be in league with the foul fiend. It is not so very long ago that all these beings, as well as elves, fairies, witches and magicians were solemnly denounced by the English clergy as allies of Satan, the great enemy of mankind.

The jinns and demons of Semitic creeds received the sanction of the Hebrew and the Christian sacred *canons*, and were fully recognized by the Rabbinic teaching, which had so vast an influence on the Christian and Mohammedan faith ; and these jinns and demons have become firmly established as the "Angels"—"the Messengers"—of the Arch-fiend.

The Titans and Rephaim, the fallen powers of heaven, furnished hierarchs for hell itself and even gave to it a monarch.

The fear engendered by superstition and ignorance : the belief in enchantment, magic, witchcraft, charms and spells : the practical fetishism which gives a spirit to every substance animate or inanimate, with power to flit from body to body,—the secret of demoniacal possession,—lie at the root of all these theories and systems, and have created and handed down all these co-operative and opposing spirits, without which the Devil himself would indeed be but a shadowy entity.

V.

THE

DEVIL'S DIVINE ANCESTORS.

The Law of Evolution—Influence of Surrounding Circumstances—
Evolution of Religious Ideals—Animism—Isolated Spirits—
Subordination of Spirits—Subjugation of Conquered Gods—
Degradation of Overpowered Gods—The Golden Age—The
Serpent—Earth Worship—Earth and Heaven combined—
Degradation of the Earth Gods—Chaldean Generation of the
Gods—Hebrew Religion — Fetishism — Slaughtering Gods—
The Serpent and Magic — Solar Deities—Rectification of
Standards of Morality—Surviving Religions—Survivals in
Christianity—Theological Criticism—Some Degraded Deities,
Bel, Zeus, Bôg, Loki, Set, Lucifer—Devas and Asuras.

THE fundamental religion of the great Turanian
race, which in primeval times overspread the whole
habitable world, was a system of animism, varying
amongst different tribes and peoples, but exhibiting
throughout a belief in all-pervading spiritual exist-
ences, which were related either to material bodies,
or to physical phenomena, past or present. The
mode in which this belief may have originated has
been discussed in the preceding chapter : it is now
proposed to examine how some of these spiritual
beings first became elevated into deities, and how in
course of time they were degraded, and became
demons or devils.

This result is due to a process of evolution, the stages of which can be traced with a fair amount of certainty.

The law of evolution, although but recently recognized and defined, has taken its place amongst the firmly established dogmas of natural science ; in the universality of its application, it ranks with the law of gravitation : it may even claim a wider range, for, whereas gravitation only affects material bodies with a dull, though steady force, evolution has been continuously at work for untold ages, not only upon every material body, but also upon the mental and moral life of man. Not only every thing, but also every idea has had its pedigree, and each link in every pedigree involves some fact of evolution. Although like produces like, likeness never amounts to identity : as circumstances successively change, and change is never absent, so successive individuals change : no son is *exactly* like his father in mind or body, and the grandson will be still less like his ancestor. No result is spontaneous, every variation is the result of heredity of one kind or another, or of some outside influence : each living organism is perpetually under influences different from those which surrounded its parents, and their offspring is not only their child, but also the child of every surrounding circumstance. The man who changes his abode from town to country, from country to town, from an alluvial

plain to a mountainous district, at once exposes his offspring to influences which tend to differentiation, and
which bring about clearly discernible modifications
in the physical system, modifications which, repeated
from generation to generation, will become more and
more pronounced and permanent.

Instead of a mere change from town to country
life, or some other slight displacement, let us suppose
a migration from one country to another, involving a
change of climate, food, pursuits, and all other physical circumstances and relations, and we shall see the
descendants of the emigrant developing characteristics which no parent or ancestor of theirs ever had,
but which are really the offspring of the outside
influences newly imported into the race, and which
thereupon modify its nature in a manner never
before experienced. Every child has three parents,
the father, the mother, and the surrounding circumstances.

The Aryas, who invaded India from the north,
were a race totally different in features and colour
from the Turanian inhabitants of the country whom
they conquered : the highest caste of the conquering
race, the Brahmans, have always been hedged round
by so many barriers against corruption of their blood,
as to make it most improbable that they should have
crossed their race with that of the dark skinned
aborigines : and yet in the south of India, under

the tropical sun, there are Brahmans as black as Pariahs. The Sanskrit name for caste is "varna," *colour :* this shows that when caste was instituted, a distinction of colour was regarded as sufficient to indicate a distinction of race : but now colour is no longer a criterion, although other features of difference are quite sufficient to attest the distinction of races.[1] It is not to be supposed for a moment that the blackness of these Brahmans was inherited from any human ancestor, it is not at all probable, nor is it necessary to so conclude : it is a matter of constant observation, that the complexion of Europeans, whose blood certainly remains unmixed with that of the native Indians, after two or three generations of residence in India, will show unmistakeable signs of darkening, and at such a rate, as to make it highly probable that a hundred generations of progress in the same direction, would find the skin completely black. Now the dark complexion, discernible in these black Brahmans, has been gradually but surely imposed upon their race by the climate and the physical circumstances in which they have been developed, and has become as much incorporated in their nature as any other characteristic passed on from father to son : so that it is impossible to lay down which of the attributes of body or mind are really

---

[1] Max Müller's " Chips," ii. 322, 323.

inherited from the first progenitors of a race, or which of them have been incorporated by such a gradual process as shown in the case of the black Brahmans. In settling any pedigree which aims at logical precision, the third parent of each link, the surrounding circumstances, must be taken into consideration.

Mr. Wallace sums up the complex nature of evolution, and the kindred process of survivals, as follows :—" If we take the organic productions of a small island, or of any very limited tract of country such as a moderate sized country parish, we have, in their relations and affinities—in the fact that they are *there* and others are *not* there, a problem which involves all the migrations of these species and their ancestral forms—all the vicissitudes of climate and all the changes of sea and land which have affected those migrations—the whole series of actions and reactions which have determined the preservation of some forms and the extinction of others—in fact the whole history of the earth, inorganic and organic, throughout a large portion of geological time."[1]

The interlacing complications involved in the evolution of physical organisms, have their exact counterparts in the evolution of human ideas ; and

---

[1] " Island Life," 6, 7.

no ideas show more distinct traces of direct descent, combined with accretions from outside and foreign influences, than those from time to time entertained respecting the deities to whom worship has been accorded by man, in the successive ages of the world.

It has been necessary to digress somewhat, in order to explain an element in evolution, which, operating more or less in all cases, is pre-eminently potent in the evolution of religions. No religion has ever, like Pallas, sprung complete from any brain, but has always been engendered by some previous ideal : all religions have been deeply tinged, and at times completely changed in character, almost beyond recognition, by their surroundings and other adventitious circumstances.

Animism, we have seen, in one form or another, was the universal religion of the primeval races of man. There was a separate spirit for each separate thing, each spirit essentially independent of all others, and only subordinated by lack of power. Professor Max Müller, borrowing an analogy from his special study of language, calls this religion " monosyllabic" :[1] Professor Haeckel, the uncompromising champion of material evolution, would call it a " one-celled" religion : and we may safely accept it as a faith founded on the realization of powers and energies,

---

[1] " Science of Religion," 155.

recognized and attributed because of their effects, but without knowledge of their causes.

The next step was the individualization of the spirits, and the attribution to them of power to pass from one substance or body to another substance or body; then the meeting of more than one spirit in the same body: rivalry for sole possession, conflict, conquest, and subordination of one spirit to another. This brought about what evolutionists call "differentiation" amongst the spirits: some classes of them were less powerful than others, and became subordinated to the more powerful classes: by the same process, these latter became ranked amongst themselves in various degrees of eminence and power, until one over-ruling head of the whole spirit world was eventually recognized. All this travelled side by side with an evolution of human society: savage man, wandering through the world to find his food, regardless of his fellows, could not long remain in that state; he must have soon learnt that absolute equality cannot exist: combination would produce a division of labour, and that subordination: subordination would develop into a state with innumerable ranks and shades of power and influence; culminating in a chief, a king, a president, a dictator, or a generalissimo. Tribes, races, kingdoms and nationalities would fight against and conquer one another; the conquering king would depose the vanquished king, and probably

consign him to chains and a dark dungeon, and his
people to slavery or tribute. The spirit world was a
reflex of the material world; and as social policy
developed with it, and when wars of races, and the
struggle for existence and supremacy arose, and political subordination ensued, the spirits and gods of the
subjugated races followed the fate of their worshippers,
and became the slaves of the conquerors' gods and
spirits, and often had to do their dirty work for them.

As physical strength and power in men was venerated and feared, so the spirits and gods were venerated and feared in proportion to the power and
strength they were believed to wield : if the gods of
Egypt were not able to nerve the Egyptians to van-
quish the Syrians, it was quite clear that the gods of
the Syrians were more powerful than those of Egypt;
and the change to a Syrian dynasty in Egypt was
logically followed by the subordination of the gods of
Egypt to those of Syria.   If at any time the gods of
Egypt enabled their people to throw off the Syrian
yoke, then it was equally logical to erase the names
of the Syrian gods from all places of honour, and
relegate them to utter darkness, like the holes and
corners where their desecrated images were thrown.
The gods are immortal, and therefore cannot die like
their analogues on earth ; but beaten, trampled down
with ignominy, expelled from heaven, and soured in
temper, their natural vocation becomes conspiracy and

revenge; the thwarting of their conqueror's plans, the undermining of his power and influence, and the compassing of his ruin, and that of all his sympathisers. Here again, man has his own experience to go by, and nothing else, and he attributes to the spirit-world motives, passions and schemes analogous to those which humans entertain and promote in parallel cases.

Power is still the test, and fear and reverence wait upon it: if power be limited or destroyed, the fear and reverence flag or die out. If the spirits of Light have conquered the spirits of the night, then in the daytime the worshippers of Light may walk secure; but when the Sun sinks in the West, and darkness steals over the earth, the spirits of darkness, like nocturnal beasts of prey, creep out of the dark holes and caves, where they had been all day companions of the moles and bats,[1] and make night hideous with their roarings; as prowling, they seek whom they may devour. Then is the time to commune with the powers of hell, and make unholy compacts for their aid to defeat virtue and the works of Light: for that is their "hour, and the *power* of darkness."[2]

It is difficult to fathom the primeval history of mankind, so as to attain reliable results. But there are nevertheless some points respecting which facts have been brought down by so many concurrent

---

[1] Isaiah ii. 20. [2] Luke xxii. 53.

H

streams of tradition, as to justify the conclusion that these traditions have some solid grounds upon which to found a theory : among such is the tradition of the Golden Age.

The Golden Age supplies the subject for a chapter in the history of almost every mythology ; a period when life was without care, and sorrows were unknown : when innocence, joy and freedom reigned supreme : when the earth produced plenty for all, and social and political strife had not been introduced into the world. This was an age of agriculture, when the earth was looked upon as the nursing mother of mankind, and of all that ministered to their comfort and well being. This was the fabled reign of Kronos amongst the Greeks, and of Saturn amongst the Latins, when Ops and Gaia were the fruitful earth, and the heavens combined with them to bring forth and ripen copious harvests. This was the early reign of the Ephesian Artemis whose attributes were those of fruitfulness. This was the age when the visible causes of reproduction and life and the earth itself were venerated as all-powerful deities, and libations and sacrifices were made to them. It was then that not only the earth, but each tree, brook, river, fountain, well, mountain, rock and stone had its spirit and received its cult.

But there was a sombre reverse to this bright and golden picture : Kronos and Saturn held the pruning knife, but it was also the sacrificial knife : the libations to the earth were of human blood, the sacrifices, human too : wherever the earth has been the supreme deity, as in the Golden Age, there have also been found the strongest belief in the efficacy and necessity of human sacrifice, and its most fanatical observance. The Khonds of India placed their earth goddess, Tari-Pennu, above the Sun-god, Boora-Pennu : their whole religion was made up of agricultural myths and rites : when Tari-Pennu had to be propitiated, it was with human victims, whose blood would fertilize the earth : in the midst of dances and drunken orgies, these victims were torn piecemeal by the frenzied worshippers and spread in morsels over their fields.[1]

Similar drunken orgies and frenzied dances were likewise the necessary accompaniments of the Kronia and Saturnalia, the festivals in which the Golden Age was specially commemorated by the Greeks and Latins, and during which mirth and pleasure were unrestrained, when master and slave laid aside all marks of distinction, and intermingled freely.

Kronos was not only the god of the Golden Age, but the devourer of his own children, like Moloch his grim Phœnician counterpart. The Ephesian Artemis, the "Diana of the Ephesians," whose

---

[1] Macpherson's "India."

worship was older than that of the Grecian Pantheon, had to be served by human sacrifices, and, although the goddess of fertility, was a dread and sombre deity. Bes, one of the oldest forms of deity found amongst the Egyptian records, was pre-eminently the slaughterer, as we find him depicted with open jaws, and a slaughtering knife in each hand. Cain also, " a tiller of the ground," did not hesitate, when he found his offerings not respected, to slay his brother Abel, in order that the earth might " open her mouth " to receive the blood.[1]

The people of the Golden Age seem to have had but little domestic strife, but this was probably because they had little or no sense of domestic virtue : they lived in herded communities inimical to moral culture ; and many strange customs, which still survive amongst savage tribes, and are even shadowed in high civilization, growing out of a low standard of morality, have relation to the state of things which existed in the primeval times of the Golden Age.

Other survivals amongst the more cultured races confirm this view : Lilith, the Rabbinic first wife of Adam, was the demoness of Lust : the Ashera, or Grove, of the Canaanitish nations, against whom such unsparing warfare was enjoined, was an

---

[1] Gen. iv.

obscene emblem, which had to be veiled, and for which the renegade Jewish women wove hangings or veils in the corrupt reign of Manasseh.[1] Besides the Saturnalia, and other popular festivals of a like nature, the primeval religion was kept in memory by various "mysteries" which, like the veiled images, were not considered fit for popular knowledge, and were either intrinsically unfit, or were such as to require special training to see the moral truth beneath an opposite presentment. The myths of Uranos and of Osiris have probably some relation to the same idea, and the modern Hindu cult of the Lingam may safely be regarded as directly brought down to the present time from the corrupt Golden Age.[2]

How or why it came about, it is difficult to determine, but it is certain that in very early ages, the serpent was generally an object of worship ; and it is probable that this worship was contemporaneous with the Golden Age. The serpent fell from his high position, but not at once ; a serpent was cursed in Eden, but seraphim—beings of a serpent form—continued to hold angelic rank, and to be the special attendants by the divine throne. The serpent as a reptile, became to the Hebrews an object of dread,

---

[1] 2 Kings xxiii. 7.

[2] See this subject elaborately worked out in Cox's "Aryan Mythology," ii. 112 et seq. And see a Paper by Mr. Sellon in the "Memoirs of the Anthropological Society," vol. 1. 327.

but it did not cease to be enjoined on them as a
model of wisdom; "Be ye wise as serpents."[1]
Amongst other nations it was the symbol of the
healing art, of life and of eternity. It is still the
object of divine worship in many parts of the world,
amongst races of Turanian origin, although in all
Aryan and Semitic religions it has become the type
of unmixed evil. The serpent-men and serpent-
women of mythology, always associated with sorcery and magic,[2] have sunk down into hell: and
although the "old serpent" was probably Ophion,
the first god of heaven, yet, as he was deposed,
discredited, and cast down into Tartaros, we accept his identification in the Apocalypse as "the
devil."[3]

Man first awoke to a sense of gratitude to unseen
powers, and to the conviction that his acts were
recognized and requited, when he found that tilling
the ground produced fertility; and that the greater

---

[1] Matt. x. 16.

[2] Before the gates there sat
On either side a formidable shape;
The one seem'd woman to the waist, and fair;
But ended foul in many a scaly fold
Voluminous and vast; a serpent arm'd
With mortal sting . . . .
. . . . . . the snaky sorceress that sat
Fast by hell-gate.—MILTON, *Paradise Lost*, ii. 648, &c.

[3] Rev. xii. 9; xx. 2 *et seq.* Lenormant's "Origines de l'Histoire," 100.

the attention paid to Mother earth, the more profuse
the benefits which she returned. His energies and
attention were therefore fixed on the earth, and whatever he gave of worship and service, was rendered to
the occult power, which in his eyes was his supreme
good. Those were the days of Eden, when the rain
from heaven did not co-operate in promoting man's
good, but the earth was watered by an earth-born moisture, for " Elohim had not caused it to rain upon the
earth, ... but there went up a mist from the earth, and
watered the whole face of the ground." [1] This was an
age of perpetual spring, when all power emanated from
the earth, and man had not been taught by hard adver-
sity, to long for the return of summer warmth, and
for the genial showers which drop fatness out of
heaven's expanse. But man and Eden parted company : man went forth to gain his bread by the
sweat of his brow, in a land of barrenness, where the
ground was cursed : Cain tilled in vain, and in vain
watered the ground with his brother's blood : the
curse was doubled, and hardship was the order of the
age : the struggle for existence became more and
more intense, and nerved the combatants to stronger
efforts, and wider fields of energy : then those who
saw that earth, unwatered by the rains of heaven,
unwarmed by the rays of the sun, was dead and

---

[1] Gen. ii. 5, 6.

unproductive; but that when the powers of the
Heavens chose to embrace the Earth, she answered
with fertility, again relapsing into dull inaction when
the Heavens withdrew their influence; they recognized that Heaven was more powerful than Earth,
and transferred their supreme allegiance to this
greater power. The stern monitor of hard facts
taught this lesson to the races, which, deprived by
expatriation, or by climatic changes, of the soft
luxurious existence of the Golden Age, were compelled to fight a desperate battle with Nature for the
means of life. In the bracing climate of the " Mountain of the World," the great Central Asian plateau,
a revolution in religious thought was being brought
about, evolved from the old ideas in combination
with the new experience of Nature's laws, or rather
of the spiritual powers which, unrecognized before,
were now found to be the greatest motors in the
world of nature. The powers of earth by no means
disappear, but they are associated with the powers
of Heaven : and this association constitutes a distinct
stage of development in a progressive course of
evolution.

We accordingly find, in the Greek mythology,
Gaea, the earth, to be the mother of Uranos, the
expanse of heaven; and that Uranos afterwards
marries his mother Gaea. The Egyptian inscriptions
bear testimony to the same paradoxical idea, for Rā

is represented as the husband of his own mother. Among the Latins, Ops, the earth, is married to Saturn : and indeed myths abound amongst all races of the marriage of heaven and earth.

But the hardy mountaineers, nurtured by an oft frowning nature ; physically, mentally and morally stronger and greater than the dwarfed and careless votaries of ease, in course of time began to pour down upon the fertile and luxuriant plains from which their ancestors had been driven. The Accadians (mountaineers) became the predominant race inhabiting the Babylonian plains, laying the foundations of the study and worship of the heavenly bodies, which developed into the Chaldean astrology and modern astronomy. Their first system of religion was dual without being exactly antagonistic, for there were spirits of the heavens, and spirits of the earth invoked in the same breath ; and although the former are evidently preferred, the latter are nevertheless great powers, deserving of worship. Other Turanian families, whose culture had developed a higher standard of thought and life, began to radiate from the centre where this culture had been nurtured, and to permeate the weaker tribes, carrying with them their religious tenets in various forms of solar worship. Such were the Phœnicians, the Etruscans, the Egyptians and the Chinese.

Later on, the Aryas, longer nurtured and hardened in their mountain home, and having developed distinctive features of body and mind, poured down into India ; and likewise, in successive waves, over-spread the whole of Europe, carrying into Greece, Italy, and Scandinavia a system of religion higher still, which, being associated with stubborn power of will, and sturdy thews and sinews, was forced upon the conquered native races, and laid the groundwork of the three great systems of Aryan mythology which have come down to our time, the Hindu, the Greek, and the Scandinavian. These systems, in India, came into contact with the oldest form of earth-worship, and probably the same was the case in some of the more favoured localities elsewhere : but the intermingling of stronger northern races had in most of these parts, already prepared the way for a transfer of supreme power from the deities of earth to those of heaven. After a period of alliance, we accordingly find the old worship relegated to ignorant, half savage country folk and rural slaves, the subjugated people ; and the gods themselves either to Tartaros, or subterranean holes and caverns : and their rites only tolerated as a con-cession to the lowest class, and made an opportunity for indulgence in the lowest vices.

However, the Greeks and Romans were an easy-going set in matters of religion : they did not object to strengthening their Pantheon with recruits from creeds and peoples of very various natures. What mattered it that there should be a score or so of extra gods, if affiliated subjects wished their deities affiliated with them. Evolution was still at work : the grub which had been born and bred in the earth, and which had fattened on the unctuous garbage of a foul and rank undergrowth, had left its earthly birthplace, had crept up between earth and heaven, and was winding itself up into an inextricable maze of philosophy, which, with all its beautiful threads of scholastic argument, could do no more than enshrine a mummied grub, the similitude of death ; for, the vitality of primeval superstition had become obscured, and nothing but scepticism or total disbelief remained.

It was reserved for another Sun, of another nature, and for the third great race of the human family, to bring about the next development of the religion of the world ; and to quicken the death-like chrysalis, to make it burst its bonds, pierce through its Dedalian envelope, and rise, the brilliant denizen of heaven's pure sky.

The religion of the Jews, at the time when it came into contact with the Greek philosophy, was essentially a·product of evolution, and the successive stages of that process of evolution can be traced with some degree of certainty, by means of the Hebrew canon, and by what can be read between the lines through the aid of contemporary history and traditions. The Genesitic accounts of the Creation, the antediluvian ages, the Deluge, and the dispersion were evidently preserved in their present form, for the purpose of enforcing what were considered the essential dogmas of the Hebrew faith, and of affording countenance to the special mode of life which the nation affected— that of a pastoral and peculiar people.

By the intermingled employment of the term Elohim, " Gods," in the plural, and of that of Jehovah, " God," in the singular, it is apparent that the early chapters of Genesis are a compilation of at least two accounts covering the same epoch, but originally written from different and somewhat inconsistent standpoints. M. François Lenormant, and other critical writers, have dissected these two versions, and fairly demonstrated the independence of their sources. Thus disentangled, the Elohistic account[1] bears a marked resemblance to the Accadian legends of the Creation and the Deluge, which the late Mr. George Smith and Professor Sayce have so ably translated and illustrated.[2] It would appear that this account, and the Chaldean legends, were derived from a common source, and it is not rash to assume that Abraham,

---

[1] F. Lenormant's " Origines de l'Histoire." Paris, 1880.
[2] Smith's "Chaldean Account of Genesis," edited by Sayce. 1880.

emigrating as he did from Ur of the Chaldees, a city
mentioned in the Accadian records, took with him
this part of the ancestral faith. The Elohim would
in that case be a group of nature gods, identified with
the assumed stages of the evolution of the material
world, and ruling the universe, each in his own department. Thus, from Abzu (the abyss) and Tiamat
(the primordial sea), had emanated Ilu "the God One,"
who gave place to a trinity of supreme gods, Anu,
the primordial Chaos, the god of time; Hea, the intelligence, the inspirer of life, the fertiliser, the king
of the element of water, "the spirit which moved on
the face of the waters," the benevolent counsellor,
the comforter; and Bel,[1] the god of the earth, the
father of the sun, moon and stars, the determiner of
destinies, "the god of the world," the god of force,
wrath and vengeance. We can here trace the stages
through which religious belief had passed before
arriving at this point: the god of the earth, the
bloody, cruel god, had preceded the heavenly hierarchy of sun, moon, and stars, which had since been
promoted to the rank of deities; for Bel, the god of
the earth, was their father.

But concurrently with the Elohim, was the great
God Jehovah, who, at first appearing in association

---

[1] This was in the early stage of development. Later on Bel
became the sun-god.

with the Chaldean Elohim, gradually becomes detached from all other conceptions of the deity, and remains the sole and the distinctive God of Israel— the only undoubted realization which history records of a "One God." And what was the Hebrew conception of their God? and whence came that conception? He was a spirit, but not that of the material earth, nor of the sun, moon or stars, nor of the sea, nor of anything that had a bodily form, or could be represented as such: but it was necessary that He should visibly *appear* in some way to His worshippers; and He accordingly revealed Himself to them in the form of Fire.

In the Jehovistic portion of Genesis, it is recorded that, on the expulsion of man from Eden, it was a flaming sword which barred his return to the tree of life—the emblem of the old religion, which was now condemned. The same account records the preference given to Abel's offering of "the firstlings of the flock, and of the *fat* thereof," which had to be burnt with fire; to Cain's offering of the "fruit of the ground" which would not be offered by fire. When the great covenant was made with Abraham,[1] and the sun had gone down, and a horror of great darkness fell upon him, Jehovah revealed Himself in "a smoking furnace, and a burning lamp that passed

---

[1] Gen. xv. 17.

between" the cloven pieces of the sacrificial victims. When the great Name was to be proclaimed, and the most ardent religion which the world has ever known was to be instituted, Jehovah revealed Himself in a burning bush. When the Israelites wandered for the forty years in the wilderness, they did so under the guidance of a pillar of fire: an appearance of fire, "the glory of Jehovah" was His manifestation in the tabernacle and the temple: when rebellion broke out in the camp, the rebels were devoured by the "fire from before Jehovah:" and when the great Mosaic law was promulgated from the brow of Sinai, "the mountain burned with fire, unto the midst of heaven, with darkness, clouds, and thick darkness," and Jehovah "spake out of the midst of the fire:"[1] "for," says the writer of the Epistle to the Hebrews, "our God is a consuming fire."[2] The whole ritual of the Levitical law involved the sacrifice by fire as the most solemn and important.

We can also, as this religion developed into a more settled form, note the extinction of some rites and customs which had characterized the superseded faith: the primeval custom referred to by Balak, and no doubt at one time universally practised, was for a man to sacrifice to his god his greatest treasure, his first-born, and perhaps his only son—the son to whom he looked to tend his sepulchre, and perform those

---

[1] Deut. iv. 11, 12.   [2] Heb. xii. 29.

funeral rites upon which alone the peace of his soul was to depend, and who would perpetuate the race for a like object. The distracted monarch inquired of the venal prophet, the dealer in maledictions, "Shall I give my first-born for my transgression, the fruit of my body for the sin of my soul?"[1] But the typical sacrifice of Isaac had been to the Hebrews the abolition of the sacrifice of the first-born to God; the circumcision of *all* the male children, and the special dedication to Jehovah of all the first-born of them and also of beasts,[2] had been a substitution for the older rite: the feast of the Passover, the destruction of all the first-born of Egypt, and the redemption by a he-lamb, roasted with fire, not raw,[3] of all the first-born of Israel, being a further confirmation of the same change.

The stern command to exterminate the Canaanitish nations, which were still addicted to the old worship, and not to intermingle with them; and also to root out sorcery and witchcraft, which were intimately associated with such worship, clearly proceeded from the same motive.

It is not difficult to detect many features in the cultured religious system of the Egyptians, which influenced, and indeed softened, that of the Hebrew; and this no doubt accounts for the general

---

[1] Micah vi. 7. [2] Exodus xiii. 12, 13. [3] Exodus xii. 9.

absence of denunciations against the Egyptian worship noticeable in the Hebrew writings.

The Hebrews, however, repeatedly reverted to the forbidden practices of the old faith, and this went on more or less until the Babylonish captivity, when contact with the highly refined system of the Persian fire worshippers, combined with the fiery trials of their captivity—passing them, as it were, through a moral and physical furnace,—purged away their corrupting dross, and sent them back to their native land with one of the purest forms of faith which the world has ever known.

Whether the Jews ever came into contact with the disciples of the Buddha it is at present impossible to say : the followers of that self-denying ascetic, from their own stand-point, certainly aimed at a purity of life and motive which could not well be rivalled ; if their influence did reach the Jews, it could only have had upon them a beneficial effect. Probably the influence, if any, did not tell until a later period of history, and affected early Christianity more than Judaism.

Even down to the Christian era the Jews, in common with the Persians, Babylonians, and others, retained distinct remnants of primeval animism, such as the belief in demons, magic, sorcery and witchcraft : and Christianity itself, the outcome of Judaism organized by Greek philosophy, has

I

never entirely shaken off the same belief, which has come down to the present day and still exists amongst us.

It is neither necessary nor desirable here to discuss such a subject as the evolution of Christianity. The history of Christianity, its doctrines and its champions ; the authenticity of its records and evidences ; its influence and its prospects ; have formed, and still form, the most voluminous subject of literature which the world has ever seen. It is sufficient to know that, as a fact, and as it now exists, the Christian religion is recognized as embodying the most enlightened system of ethics, and the purest moral code, that have ever been promulgated ; and that in comparison with its light, all other systems appear in semi or complete obscurity.

Mohammedanism, Confucianism and Buddhism all boast a standard of moral excellence worthy of comparison with that of Christianity, and the boasting is not wholly vain ; passages in ancient records of Egypt, Assyria, and in the Greek and Latin classics, attest that light was never absent from the cultured races : and the touching child-like faith of many a savage race of modern times, reflecting as it undoubtedly does, much that has always been common in such races, show that veneration, faith and charity have always existed, sufficient to furnish a ground-work for the development of those higher

DEPOSED DEITIES

systems, which are now regarded as representing the highest good.

But the passage from the Earth to Heaven, which the human mind has made, has been like an aërial ascent, in which, at every stage, it has been necessary to cast out the earthy ballast which dragged man down. As faith soared into purer light, these weights were cast adrift, and, being left behind, appeared like earthly things ; although the time was when they were seen as bright lights, shining in the heavens. Man's gaze is upwards, and when he glances down below, from the point he has attained he sees the things he cast away—his stepping-stones to light—as plunged in sombre gloom, and, forgetful of their history, despises them.

The first outcome of animism was fetishism, arising from the belief that a material body was necessary for every soul or spirit, and that, when a soul or spirit found itself disembodied, it was rest-less, intractable, and incapable of communication with material man ; and, at most, could only appear to him in dreams and trances. Something of this idea is discernible in the Odyssey, where the unsub-stantial shades of the departed are described as incapable of rational action, until feasted on the life-blood of the recently slain victims :—

All pale ascends my royal mother's shade :
A queen of Troy she saw her legions pass ;
Now a thin form is all Anticlea was !
Struck at the sight I melt with filial woe,
And down my cheek the pious sorrows flow,
Yet as I shook my falchion o'er the blood,
Regardless of her son the parent stood.

But say why yonder on the lonely strands,
Unmindful of her son, Anticlea stands ?

Know ; to the spectres, that thy bev'rage taste,
The scenes of life recur, and actions past ;
They, seal'd with truth, return the sure reply ;
The rest, repell'd, a train oblivious fly.

When near Anticlea moved and drank the blood
Straight all the mother in her soul awakes.[1]

According to Arabian legends, the Jinns were spirits created without bodies, and are supposed to be perpetually wandering about to find bodies to inhabit ; and Asmodeus, the demon of lust, seeks to enter human bodies, in order to give himself up to carnal enjoyments.

The savage mind, believing in the existence of myriads of souls or spirits, saw no objection to several spirits inhabiting the same body or substance, and passing freely from one to another. It became, therefore, a matter of great importance to cause, if

---

[1] "Odyssey," b. 11.

possible, the right spirit to be in the right substance, so as to either utilize its power for good, or to neutralize its malignant powers. If a man was ill of a fever, he was deemed to be possessed by a fever demon ; the desideratum then was to get some propitious and stronger demon to enter the man's body and expel the fever demon. From this belief the doctrines of demoniacal possession, spiritual inspiration, exorcism by incantations, and the laying of spirits, had their rise. It was firmly believed that if the proper forms were used, a spirit could be isolated in a substance, like electricity in a Leyden jar, and that the operator could then, at will, wield the spirit's power, and discharge it in any desired direction.

This principle being firmly established, then everything having a material existence was capable of being a fetish, and subserving the will of any one having power over the possessed matter : animals, trees, stocks and stones were recognized as fetishes at an early stage ; particularly famous trees, strange or intelligent animals, stones that had fallen from heaven, like the aërolite, in which Artemis of the Ephesians was believed to reside : even now the African negroes and other tribes worship the stone hammers and arrow-heads, relics of the stone age, the origin of which is forgotten, under the impression that they dropped from heaven, and must therefore contain some powerful spirit.

But man in time required something more realistic than an upright block of wood, or a boulder, as the embodiment of his constant allies, the spirits ; and he began to shape his fetish in accordance with his notion of the spirits' forms and attributes ; the spirits were in general those of his ancestors, and traditions of men of low stature, with coarse strong limbs and open mouths thirsting for blood, rejoicing in slaughter and the effusion of blood, and promoting that end to the utmost of their power, was naturally the conception formed of those early ancestors. We therefore find the dumpy semi-bestial, open-mouthed figure of Bes, with a slaughtering knife in each hand as an image of a demon deity, furnished, too, with a tail, whether from supposition, or from a tradition that the remote ancestor rejoiced in that ornament, it is now impossible to say. If the king of Dahomey should come to be represented in his true character by some pious descendant, he would be not inaptly modelled like Bes, minus the tail. Destruction is a frantic joy accompanying a low and brutal nature : the blood-thirsty savage gloats over a score of victims set in a row for him to decapitate ; the Assyrian conqueror's reward for all the hardship and risk of a campaign, was the power of hacking down the fettered prisoners of war until the physical power to slaughter was exhausted : and there is a survival of the same passion when a modern " sportsman " spends quite a

fortune in rearing vast numbers of birds, so that he
may be able to take the greatest number of lives, in
the shortest possible time, and with the least possible
exertion ; or where the felling of a tree or the slashing
of railway cushions is a special treat after grand
exertions in politics or business.[1]

As time went on the sacrificial slaughter of human
victims, and the probable accompaniment of cannibal-
ism, became abated, the savage slaughtering gods
fell into disrepute, were looked upon with abhorrence,
and at last became the recognized ideal of evil. The
obscene and brutal Bes, Kronos, who devoured his
own children, and Moloch, who consumed those of
others, thus became demons, and were relegated to
Tartaros.

The serpent, however much it was considered to
be wise, was by its very nature a subject of intense
fear. It was small but powerful, and, looked upon
as a fetish, its possessing spirit could exert its
power with dire effect. Great effectual power, combined with small physical strength, created an idea
of cunning akin to that of sorcery. Long after
other systems of fetish worship had fallen into
desuetude, the veneration for the serpent, fed by fear,

---

[1] The author was once authentically assured that a certain mem-
ber of the swell-mob, whenever successful in an important swindle,
treated himself to a first-class railway journey in order that he might
destroy the railway cushions, and thus give vent to the exuberance
of his spirits.

survived ; and the form of the serpent passed on from age to age as an accompaniment of magical power. We thus find on the Chaldean seals serpents and scorpions —and in all sorts of mythologies women with serpent tails or serpent hair, or both, who wield some magic power : Lilith, the Hebrew sorceress, rival and enemy of Eve, had a woman's body and a serpent's tail.   The serpent's reputation was of long duration, even amongst the Hebrews, and died hard in the days of Hezekiah, when the brazen serpent of the wilderness was finally ground to dust, called "Nehushtan," and dispersed.   Amongst the serpent worshipping tribes of India and many other races, and even in Brahmanism, the serpent has retained its prestige, but amongst Jews, Mohammedans and Christians, it has been most thoroughly demonized, and the deities whose attributes were connected with the serpent have generally shared the same fate.

Amongst solar deities there has been a great subsidence into the realms of darkness ; but, except in comparatively few instances, the degradation has not been so complete as with their predecessors in popular favour ; possibly because solar worship itself was not necessarily degrading, except so far as it represented the deification of an error, or so far as demoralizing customs, superstitions and rites were inherited from the superseded forms of worship, and incorporated with that of the sun.   The earliest solar deities seem to have been of the hero type, such as Nimrod, the mighty hunter; Izdhubar, the mass of fire,—the Accadian fire-god,—and Adonis; all of whom being of mixed human and divine origin, were of too material a nature to withstand the degradation which was sure to be involved by their very human passions, inconsistent with the purity to which solar worship in course of time was raised. The cruel Bel, who caused the Deluge, and wished to destroy even the few survivors, was too cruel a god to remain in heaven: and even Osiris, the supreme deity of the most idealized form of the sun god, upon whom were fixed the hopes of all the devout Egyptians, whose code of morality is almost a counterpart of that of the Christian, has found his place in the realms of Satan: whilst Mercury, or Hermes, the messenger of the gods, and the mediator for men in Hades, has drifted into the same company, whilst, as Michael, the Archangel, he has retained his place in heaven.

In the early ages of the human race, when man's ideal of perfection was based on the life and habits of his own ancestors, who were really less enlightened than himself; when Nature was so little understood, and power was the great insignia of deity, the characters attributed to the gods were too much chequered with good and evil, and the standards of human right and wrong—of human good and evil—were necessarily too confused to remain unchanged when man's ideal became more elevated : they required continual rectification, to satisfy the human mind in its more cultured state : and as it discerned a truer basis for the general welfare, and science unfolded its truths, this rectification silently but surely followed.

The philosophical systems of the Greeks and Romans, and earlier still, those of the Egyptians and Assyrians, settled standards of morality for the regulation of every-day life, which were certainly purer than could have been expected from the traditional lives of the deities whom they worshipped : for those deities belonged to an earlier age of greater ignorance, and coarser habits of life. The consequence was a tendency, more and more pronounced, either to discredit the deities, or to explain away their histories, by allegorizing them : it being impossible to apply reasonably to daily life the principles attributed to the gods. For the same reason the rude, uncouth and obscene images of the oldest gods had to be veiled, and only remained gods when enveloped in mystery. By degrees the gods either ceased to be believed in, or became resolved into solar and other natural myths, and their anthropomorphic acts were interpreted as the mere poetical exposition of the cosmical forces in Nature. In this way the school of the Euhemerists reduced the romantic mythology of Greece to the most prosaic series of common-place incidents.

This view, however, was only realized by a comparative few, the philosophers and men of culture of the time, who took the trouble to think the subject out: the old mythology still existed, inextricably woven into the life of the people: there were moreover episodes in this mythology, which represented the gods not only as accessible, but as continually yielding to sensual and vindictive passions; this struck a chord of sympathy in the habits and tastes of all but the highly cultured, and it became impossible to destroy the ancient deities, and wipe out their memory and worship from the popular life; from age to age they lingered on, changed, distorted, and defamed, plunged into darkness and disrepute, but neither dead nor out of mind, and they are still alive: truly they are the " immortal gods !"

This process had been going on for ages before the Christian era, but since Christianity has attained preponderating influence, and been supported by secular authority, the gods of the ancients have been finally degraded into devils, and indiscriminately cast down to Hell.

The cultured missionary apostle of Christianity wrote "the Gentiles sacrifice to devils, and not to God."[1] From a Christian point of view this was true; for the heathen gods had been denounced as

---

[1] I Cor. x. 20.

evil demons in disguise. But St. Paul in fact only echoed the prevailing philosophy of his time which had become entirely detached from the popular deities, who were only fitted to assist and screen the dishonest and dissolute, or at most to furnish poetical tropes and figures. In result, almost all the distinctive names, which are now applied and which have been applied to the devil, can be traced to the name of some high god, in his time worshipped and revered by some people or other, with all the devotion of which they were capable. Milton, who certainly reflects the orthodox belief on this subject of the Christian age in which he lived, has shown us Moloch, Beelzebub, Lucifer, Baal, Astarte, Adonis, Tammuz, Rimmon, Osiris, Horus and Serapis, wallowing in the fiery lake of Hell, although they formerly were—

> Princes, Potentates,
> Warriors, the flower of Heaven !

But they had changed :—

> They but now who seem'd
> In bigness to surpass earth's giant sons,
> Now less than smallest dwarfs in narrow room
> Throng numberless, like that Pygmëan race
> Beyond the Indian mount; or faery elves,
> Whose midnight revels, by a forest side
> Or fountain, some belated peasant sees,
> Or dreams he sees.[1]

---

[1] Milton, " Paradise Lost ;" b. i.

The poet at the same time, for the purpose of his epic, but also in accordance with venerable tradition, explains that these gods were originally preadamite demons ; and that they became missionaries from Hell, and entered into the false gods, whose names they bore, in order to bring about the corruption of man, the last and best created handiwork of Jehovah, the Creator.

The religions of the present day which have the most vitality, are those which have raised the Deity to the highest position of ideal purity, and have bereft Him almost entirely of human attributes. We still however see the battle between idealism and realism going on, and the dangers of each. The Brahman system was realistic in the extreme ; Buddhism cast off the earthly coil, aimed at ideal purity, and set before its disciples the final goal of nothingness, annihilation—Nirvāna—as the supreme good.[1] The Brahmans had proceeded on an error, in assuming the unending transmigration of souls ; and the Buddha had invented Buddhism as a means to attaining annihilation in order to escape these weary cycles. This marvellous system of virtuous

---

[1] The object of all the asceticism of the Buddhist religion was "Simply to guide each individual towards that path which would finally bring him to 'Nirvāna,' to utter extinction or annihilation, to cross over to the other shore which was not death, but cessation of all being."—MAX MÜLLER'S *Chips*, i. 248.

self abnegation consequently proceeded in like manner upon an erroneous foundation; although its high standard of Faith, Hope, and Charity could not fail to command respect: the aim was sublime, but it missed its mark: the Buddhist creed has either evaporated through transcendentalism into an absence of all belief, ending in blank materialism: or it has drifted back into the narrow superstitions of Brahmanism. The spirit worship of the Chinese became moralized by Confucius, but could not stand the transformation, and Taoism, the most degraded form of Buddhism, is the outcome. Mohammedanism has stood the test of many a hard battle, and for the peoples whom it sways, it is a vital and, on the whole, a beneficial power: there are not wanting amongst us prophets who proclaim renewed vigour and increased influence to the faith of Islam: but the contact with western civilization, and the deadening influence which contact and sympathy with other successful systems produce, are certainly eating into and permeating the doctrines of the Prophet. Christianity, the most restless of all creeds, with every range of culture within its pale, presents the best examples of the evolution of religious belief:—a Christian may believe in the importation of a spirit into a substance or person by means of a form of words, he may also believe in exorcism; he habitually recognizes the presence of spirits in certain special places ; thereby rendering homage to the doctrines of Fetishism :—he may readily adopt the figurative language of the East, and address the deity in words not distinguishable from solar invocations ; and thereby follow the very language of the worshippers of Osiris and Bel, of Apollo and Tammuz :—he may venerate saints, martyrs, prophets, virgins and confessors ; the ancestral spirits of a past gone age; and thereby illustrate a full, developed and vigorous manes-worship, without transgressing the strictest rules of the Christian faith. If he discard all these, and centre his ideal on an abstract essence of good, untouched and unsurrounded by any material attribute, he is at once in danger of finding his own faith evaporate with his ideal—and of waking up from his trance a materialist and nothing else. The dangers are still alternative of overmuch superstition or of too little belief.

Seen from a Christian point of view, Buddhism, Mohammedanism, and the religions of China are overlaid with superstitions and fallacies to such an extent as to unfit them for control over the human judgment: but if Christianity, and the practical effect which it has upon the lives and conduct of its professors be intelligently examined and criticised by an educated disciple of the Buddha, or of Confucius, he would find much to cavil at, and his theological opponents would find it somewhat difficult to reply. It is said that a missionary of Confucianism recently demonstrated to an American audience, that the doctrines of Confucius had a far greater influence than the teaching of Christianity to prevent crime and the neglect of family and domestic duties.

It is so difficult to approach any question judicially, and most so when the question is deemed of such paramount importance as that of the welfare of immortal souls, that no one brought up and educated in a Christian community can easily bring himself to look at these matters with a totally unprejudiced mind : but a few historical facts will demonstrate the great and radical changes of opinion which earnest and honest believers have in former times passed through. We will now refer to a few instances in which former deities can be shown to have become degraded and converted into devils.

Bel was the supreme deity of the Assyrians, and probably of all the Semitic races; originally the demiurges, he in course of time became more exclusively identified with the sun in his glory, as quickener of nature, the great Creator, and the source of light and life. His Syrian counterpart was Baal, and in one form, in relation to his influence over flies, was known as Baal-Zebul. The Hebrews, first by a pun changed his name to Beel-Zebub (dung-god), and afterwards crowned him " the Prince of Devils."

The Greek Zeus, the Latin Deus, and many other modifications of the same original root, run through all the Aryan forms of speech, as the title of the supreme god, the original root meaning "the Shining One." Our word "deuce," which means "a little devil," is the vernacular representative of this venerable root.

The Sclavonic word for god is "Bôg;" this word also has run through a marvellous number of modifications, having kindred significations, but it has finished with us in the name of "Bogie."[1]

Loki, the Scandinavian devil, who is now indentified with Satan, is the German "Leucht," or Light: he was more mischievous than malevolent, and can without difficulty be identified with Hermes and Mercury, the messengers—the Angels—of Zeus and Jupiter—the rays proceeding from the great light of heaven. Loki is thus described in the prose Edda: "There is another deity reckoned in the number of the Æsir, whom some call the calumniator of the gods, the contriver of all fraud and mischief, and the disgrace of gods and men : his name is 'Loki' or Loptur. . . . . Loki is handsome and well made, but of a very fickle mood, and most evil disposition. He surpasses all beings in those arts called cunning and perfidy. Many a time has he exposed the gods

---

[1] Baring-Gould, "Religious Belief," 98.

to very great perils, and often extricated them again by his artifices."[1]   Although now a devil, he was once among the Æsir, the great gods of the Scandinavian Olympos.

Set was the devil of the later Egyptian mythology : " Set, though the antagonist of Light in the myths of Rā, Osiris and Horus, is not a god of evil.   He represents a physical reality, a constant and everlasting law of Nature, and is as true a god as his opponents.   His worship is as ancient as any.   The kings of Egypt were as devoted to Set as to Horus, and derived from them the sovereignty over north and south.   On some monuments one god is represented with two heads, one being that of Horus, the other that of Set.   The name of the great conqueror, ' Seti,' signifies ' he that is devoted to Set.'   It was not till the decline of the Empire that this deity came to be regarded as an evil demon, that his name was effaced from monuments, and other names substituted for his in the Ritual."[2]

Lucifer is referred to in Isaiah xii. 14 as " son of the morning," and clearly signifies a " bright star," and probably what we call the morning star. The Christian church from St. Jerome downwards has identified Satan with this Lucifer, probably

---

[1] Mallet's " Northern Antiquities," 422.
[2] Renouf's " Hibbert Lectures," 1879, 117.

because Lucifer having been a Babylonish deity, the fall of the Babylonish Empire has been taken as analogous to the fall of Satan from heaven.[1] Lucifer seems to have lost his character through a figure of speech.

The religious system of Persia affords a most striking instance of deities originally adored being degraded into devils. This system records the great conflict between Ormuzd and Ahriman, Light and Darkness, the good and evil principles : but another conflict equally violent has been enacted on the great field of Aryan theology, one result of which is that the word " deva," originally signifying " a bright one," and still meaning a deity to Brahmans, is " a devil" to Parsees. On the other hand the " Ahuras" of the Parsees are gods, Ahura-mazdu (Ormuzd) is their supreme god ; yet the same word " Asuras" in the Hindu means malignant demons. The bitterness of some theological controversy of a long bygone age, or some internecine war, at a time when the Iranian and the Aryan had not parted company,—perhaps the feud which brought about the separation,—bore its usual fruit : each party, with the virulent implacability which characterizes religious discord, branded its opponents as devil worshippers : and now that the din of battle is

---

[1] Smith's " Dictionary of the Bible," tit. " Lucifer."

hushed, mutual persecution ended, and even the motive cause forgotten, it appears that *all* the gods of each party, have, by one side or the other, been torn from their celestial thrones, and contemptuously thrust down to Hell to rank as devils.

Similar instances might be multiplied, taken from the history of every creed and nation, but the position is sufficiently illustrated by the fact, that Beelzebub, Lucifer, Loki, Set and the Deuce have each in his time sat high among the gods, and as they all must be ranked as ancestors of the modern devil, it may fairly, and indeed literally be said that " Satan has fallen from Heaven."

VI.

HELL AND ITS MONARCHS.

Hell — Hades, the Invisible World — Bit-Hadi — 'Aides — Sheol —
    Assyrian Hades — Allat — Greek Hades and Tartaros — Minos
    — Egyptian Hall of Two Truths — Plato's Hades — Ovid's
    Hades — Virgil's Regions — Rabbinical Ideas — Gehenna — Judges
    in Hades.

THE Devil is regarded as the Monarch of Hell, and
Hell is conceived with more or less vagueness as
a place of retribution "prepared for the devil and his
angels."[1] There was a time when the place now
called Hell was presided over by the highest, the
most moral god which at the time was acknowledged.
The god of Hell now is undoubtedly the Devil,
Satan.

Theologians of the present day do not define what
Hell is; they speak of the older descriptions as
figurative, and dilate upon its moral horrors and
torments, as represented by the physical sufferings
and dread gloom recorded by earlier writers. Only
the ignorant addressing the ignorant, in solemn

---

[1] Matt. xxv. 41.

earnest; or poets appealing to the emotions of the imaginative, in measured rhythm, place before their hearers or their readers the harrowing details of fire and brimstone, darkness and chains, which formed so large a staple of the teaching in medieval times.

The purity of Milton's style, and the refinement of his thought, have furnished an exact ideal of the Hell of the later Christian period, before it melted into a mere unsubstantial expression :—

> A dungeon horrible, on all sides round,
> As one great furnace, flamed; yet from those flames
> No light; but rather darkness visible
> Served only to discover sights of woe,
> Regions of sorrow, doleful shades, where peace
> And rest can never dwell; hope never comes
> That comes to all; but torture without end
> Still urges, and a fiery deluge, fed
> With ever-burning sulphur unconsumed.[1]

This Hell has had its pedigree, its earliest ancestor being a product of necessity, the obvious outcome of animistic belief: animistic belief being almost universal, the belief in an invisible world, inhabited by invisible beings, became equally general.

The idea was that there are two great co-existing worlds, the visible, material world, and the unseen spiritual world; the earth, the material world in

---

[1] Milton's, "Paradise Lost," b. i.

which we live, is specially associated with the state in which men's bodies exist; Hades, the unseen world, is the abode of all the disembodied souls of all past generations: the earth is the abode of one generation of living bodies; Hades that of the souls of all the generations, which, since the world began, have lived their mortal lives and passed away: Hades is therefore necessarily a place of vast extent and great importance, and any Being believed to be invested with the sovereignty of that unseen world, has had a realm which could not be considered as less important, than that over the one, short-lived, passing generation of mortal men. Where the immortality of the soul, and its non-return to a material existence, were received as dogmas, the God of the unseen world became supereminently great.

The primary meaning of the word Hades is simply "Invisible":—men died, their souls quitted their bodies, and became invisible, they had entered invisibility, Hades; but terms such as these oft repeated, and having a defined meaning, soon become materialized: ideas are like the Rabbinical demons,[1] always seeking for bodies to inhabit, and not long remaining disembodied; and in the present case, the expression invisible had a fabric appropriated for it, not only a name but also a local habitation, which in course of time became very real and definite indeed.

----

[1] See p. 53.

It is not proposed here to discuss the wide subject of primeval belief in a future life, and the great variety of views on this subject known to have been and to be still entertained by different races of men. As before pointed out, some belief of the sort.was a necessary corollary of the belief in souls and spirits, and in effect we find some such belief almost universal. The first form which it assumed was that of a future state of all alike in which, with more or less of conscious individuality, the present life was continued in the next. Sometimes the mode of life on earth influenced the soul's fate in the next, but that was hardly the primitive idea. The standard of good and evil in this life was but very confused, and the sanction of such a standard did not reach beyond the grave.

Then, as to the place fixed for Hades, opinions varied extremely ; it was beyond the seas, or in the heavens, or the sun, or the moon, or under the earth. The most generally adopted view, and that which has come down to modern days with the greatest force, is that Hades is below the earth, and that it is reached over the waters of a river or ocean, which has come to be called the river of Death.

This abode of the dead at first had a shadowy, unsubstantial, cold existence, where the shades were without blood or warmth, melancholy, whistling whiffs of air, whose teeth chattered or gnashed with the cold, as they swept through the outer darkness. This was the mournful gloom, and the chill, dark melancholy of the tomb, or sepulchral cave : the " Bit-Hadi, the house of Eternity," of the old Assyrian tablets. It does not seem improbable that this term " *Hadi*," signifying " Eternity," was the original name brought from the East, and that *'aides*, Hades, invisible, was adopted as an after-thought as being equally appropriate to the subject.[1]

The Accadian Hades, as mentioned in the tablet records, probably the oldest in the world, is of this negative kind, it is a " place where no feeling exists, the foundation of chaos, the place where there is no blessing, the tomb, the place where no one can see, the abode of confusion ;" nevertheless reigned over by a ruler, " Nin-ge, upon her raised altars," with her spouse Mul-ge.[2] It is described as the abyss of Hades, the offspring of the chaos of primeval waters.[3]

The Hades of the ancient Hebrews was called " Sheol," and probably owed its origin to the same source as that of the Accadians or Chaldeans. The word Sheol means a " hollow-place," representing the same idea as " Hölle," " a hole, a hollow place," the original form of the English word " Hell."

Sheol was the destination of all the dead whether

---

[1] " Transactions Bib. Arch." ii. 188.

[2] Lenormant's " Chaldean Magic," 166. 170.

[3] " Records of the Past," ix. 117.

good or bad ; the patriarch Jacob looked forward to going there,[1] Job prayed to be sent there,[2] and the wicked are turned into it;[3] it is never full and is insatiable ;[4] it is the abode of the departed Rephaim, the Hebrew Titans, who have become weak and trembling, and who shudder when Jehovah's eye pierces through the accustomed gloom.[5]   In these very earliest types there is no trace of Hades being a place of punishment, beyond the fact that a speedy or premature devotion to Sheol, involving earthly death, was looked upon as a form of retribution to the wicked.

The Assyrian Hades, as described in the account of Istar's descent into Hades, although in the main a sombre abode of listless emptiness, like the Hebrew Sheol, had developed a department of judgment, followed by personal punishment or reward, which constitutes a most important variation, perpetuated and further developed in after times. It is a land of darkness, from which light is excluded and is never seen, a road from which there is no return, a place where its chiefs are like hovering birds who do not even disturb the dust which remains on the doors and bolts ; where the dead would fain escape to devour the living ; but they cannot, for it is a house out of which there is no

---

[1] Gen. xxxvii. 35.   [2] Job. xiv. 13.   [3] Ps. ix. 17.
[4] Prov. xxvii. 20 ; xxx. 16.   [5] Is. xiv. 10 ; Job xxvi. 5, 6.

exit, and dust is their nourishment, and their food
mud. The entrance is guarded by the keeper of the
waters, who demands from all comers homage for
Allat the queen of Hades : each comer is then spell-
bound and passes successively through seven gates,
at each of which some of the glories and pomps of
life fall off, so that on reaching the presence of Allat
nothing is left, and even the power to speak is gone.
But beyond these death-like characteristics, there are
others of a life-like kind : even in that age, one
looking forward to this valley of the shadow of death
could say :—

> In the house, O my friend, which I will enter,
> For me is treasured up a crown ;
> With those wearing crowns who from days of old ruled the
> earth,
> To whom the gods Anu and Bel have given names of rule.
> Water they have given to quench the thirst, they drink
> limpid waters.
> In the house, O my friend, which I will enter,
> Dwell the lord and the unconquered one,
> Dwell the priest and the great man.[1]

In this Assyrian Hades, we read that at the command of Allat, the spirits of the earth come forth,
and are seated on thrones of gold ; the ashêrim, the
symbols of the ancient earth goddess Ashârah (the
grove) are adorned with precious stones,—the tree

---

[1] Smith, " Genesis," Sayce, 236.

of life bears its twelve kinds of gem-like fruit, the
waters of life are given, and the seven gates of Hades
reopen for a triumphant exit with renovated glory.[1]
This is a veritable doctrine of future life and resur-
rection. But if she can dispense rewards, Allat can
also condemn, and the task seems a congenial one to
her. She can strike eyes, side, feet, heart, head and
the whole body with disease : she will consign to
the great prison, with garbage for food, drains for
drink, dungeon darkness for dwelling, a stake for
seat, and with hunger and thirst for attendants.[2]
Here we have future retribution framed on the model
of earthly punishment in its then accustomed form.

One step further in the development of the idea
of Hades brings us to the conception of the early
Greeks on the subject, as systematically stated
by Hesiod, and graphically described by Homer
in the Odyssey—Hesiod, who personifies all places
and phenomena, makes Hades the brother of Zeus,
marries him to Persephone, and describes their
realm in gloomy depths below the earth, vaulted
in by huge rocks, at the sources and boundaries
of dusky earth, and murky Tartaros, and barren
sea,   and   starry   heaven,   boundaries   oppressive
and gloomy which even gods abhor. This is surrounded by the river Styx, which is a tenth part of

---

[1] Smith, " Genesis," Sayce, 244.
[2] *Ib.* and see further " Trans. Bib. Arch." iv. 288.

the wide ocean turned back into the bowels of the earth to encircle the land of shades, a stream of fate which even the Olympian gods cannot disregard with impunity. Below all this in the deepest depths is a dark drear place, Tartaros, oppressive and gloomy, walled in with double walls, and closed above with brazen gates; so deep that a brazen anvil dropped from earth would fall nine days and nights and only reach it on the tenth; a vast chasm, in which, with perpetual whirlwinds, one would be for a whole year driven round and round without reaching the pavement. Here the enemies of God, the Titans, the fallen angels of Greek mythology, were for their rebellion doomed to ruthless punishment. If any of the great gods forswore themselves: on the waters of the Styx, they were condemned to Tartaros by an inexorable fate stronger than themselves, a first year passed in breathless stupor, was followed by nine years of ever increasing trouble, until ten years of punishment and famine wiped out the dire offence, and made them fit again to return to Olympos, and take part in the councils and feasts of the gods.

The Odyssey gives us more details of the realms of death. At old ocean's utmost bounds, where the dusky nation of Cimmeria dwells, where the sun never shines, and endless night and clouds of dull air envelop them in shades, are the cavernous passages to the infernal regions. Sacrifices and invoca-

tions bring up from below vast shoals of thin, airy,
visionary ghosts, shrieking and trembling, who crowd
round the slain victims, and seek to drink the blood.
A waving falchion wards them off. The few who are
allowed to drink regain their consciousness: the
others, impassive souls, reluctant fly, like a vain
dream, through the dolesome realms of darkness and
of death,—a dire region, where lakes profound
and floods oppose their waves, where the wide sea
with all its billows raves.

All this is the old idea of Sheol, but there are
other scenes than this :—

> High on a throne tremendous to behold,
> Stern Minos waves a mace of burnish'd gold :
> Around ten thousand thousand spectres stand
> Thro' the wide dome of Dis, a trembling band.
> Still as they plead, the fatal lots he rolls,
> Absolves the just, and dooms the guilty souls.[1]

We are then told of demigods suffering an everlasting penance, and we are led to understand that
" the kings of ancient days, the mighty dead that live
in endless praise," could be seen, and assumedly in
good case, but the narrator is cut short by swarms of
spectres which rise from deepest hell, with bloodless
visage and with hideous yell, they scream, they
shriek, sad groans and dismal sounds stun his scared
ears, and pierce hell's utmost bounds: he cannot
sustain the din and hurries back to the upper air.

---

[1] " Odyssey," b. 11.

All these forms of Hades partake very largely of the primeval ideas connected with the shades of the departed, and only incidently recognize accountability after death for the deeds done in the body. This latter conception belongs to a high state of culture and its development can be traced alongside of the development of such culture. This cannot be better illustrated than by a reference to the tenets of the ancient Egyptians upon the subject of the future life. They believed that at death the soul and body separated, and whilst the body was being ferried over the Nile, and entombed with funereal pomp and ritual of a most elaborate nature, the soul entered the realms of the underworld and was ferried over the infernal Nile, ushered into the hall of the Two Truths, there to undergo a formal trial, and receive a doom in direct relation to the moral conduct in the earthly life as ascertained by the judges.

The journey to the hall of judgment is one beset with terrors of every kind, which the deceased must encounter—gigantic and venomous serpents, gods with names significant of death and destruction, waters and atmospheres of flames, beds of torment, nets and devouring monsters. The wicked who succumb are said to undergo "the second death;" but the faithful dead expect to be protected from all these dangers, partly by amulets and talismans of magic power, partly by the knowledge of religious

formulas (such as the chapters of the Book of the
Dead) and of divine names, but chiefly by the conformity of their conduct with the standard of law by
which they are judged in the Hall of the Two Truths.
Arrived at the Hall, the soul is conducted by
Horus into the presence of Osiris his father, presiding
over a court composed of forty-two assessors, who
adjudicate with him on the life and actions of the
deceased. This trial turns upon points of morality
of which no religious system need be ashamed. The
inquiry is whether the professions put into the
deceased's mouth are correct or not : " I have not
blasphemed, I have not cheated, I have not stolen, I
have not caused strife, I have treated ʻno one with
cruelty, I have occasioned no disorders, I have not
been an idler, I have not been given to drunken-
ness, I have given no unjust orders, I have not been
indiscreet through idle curiosity, I have not indulged
in vain talk nor in evil speaking, I have used violence
to no one, I have caused no one to fear unjustly, I
have not been envious, I have never spoken evil of
the king nor of my parents, I have not brought
any false accusation. I have made the requisite
offerings to the gods, for the love of God I have
given food to the hungry, drink to the thirsty,
clothing to the naked, and shelter to the destitute."[1]

---

[1] " Chrestos," by Dr. Mitchell, 25, 26.

At the termination of the hearing, at which Horus assists as a mediator and pleads his own good works for the vicarious benefit of the deceased, the good actions of the deceased are placed in one scale of a balance, and the emblem of truth in the other, and Osiris pronounces judgment according to the result.   If the deceased's good actions are sufficiently weighty, he is awarded admission to heaven, and the enjoyment of eternal felicity.   If on the other hand he is found wanting, he is condemned to return to the earth in the form of a pig, or some other unclean animal, there to go through a fresh term of life ; or he may be condemned to a term of purification in Purgatory, for the judgment hall has three openings, one into *Aalu*, heaven, a second into *Karr*, hell, and a third into *Ker-neter*, purgatory.[1]

The constant intercommunication between Egypt and Greece, could not fail to produce a marked effect upon the superstitions of the latter on the important subject of future life ; and we accordingly find, that the region of Hades described by the earlier poets, is rectified so as to bring it more into conformity with the advanced and refined ideal of the Egyptians. On arriving at the asphodel meadow, within the gates of Death, the soul sees three judges sitting to decide its fate : Eacus to try those from Europe, Rhadamanthus, those from Asia, and Minos, as

---

[1] Renouf's " Hibb. Lectures," 1879.

referee, in case of doubt; two roads turn off from here, the one to the isles of the blessed, the other to Tartaros: those who are condemned to the latter are so condemned for their sins committed in the flesh; if the offence be curable, the punishment awarded has amendment for its object; and if incurable, then the punishment is for ever, as examples, for a spectacle of warning to unjust men.[1] Tartaros is the one place of punishment for both classes of offenders, but each suffers only according to his deserts. This subject is fully worked out by Plato, who puts the explanation into the mouth of Socrates, as an argument for a virtuous and pious life ending in a peaceful death.

Ideas upon the subject of Hades were being collected by philosophers and poets, and the process of evolution was as usual advancing from the more simple, to the more complicated and detailed. The Romans absorbed the Greek learning on the subject, and no doubt affiliated many another notion culled from the corners of their vast and growing empire.

Ovid in a few words described the Hades of the Romans: "There is a shelving path, shaded with dismal yew, which leads through profound silence to the infernal abodes. Here languid Styx exhales vapours; and the new-made ghosts descend this way,

---

[1] Plato, Gorgias.

HADES

and phantoms when they have enjoyed funereal rites. Horror and winter possess these dreary regions far and wide, and the ghosts newly arrived know not where the way is that leads to the Stygian city, or where is the dismal palace of the black Pluto. The wide city has a thousand passages, and gates open on every side. And as the sea receives the rivers for the whole earth, so does that spot receive all the souls; nor is it too little for any amount of people, nor does it perceive the crowd to increase. The shades wander about, bloodless, without body and bones; and some throng the place of judgment; some the abode of the infernal prince. Some pursue various callings, in imitation of their former life; their own punishment confines others."[1]

No classic writer, however, has entered into such minute details of the infernal regions as Virgil, and from him we learn that the whole nether world called Orcus is divided into five regions :—

1. *The Previous Region.*
2. *The Watery Region—The Styx.*
3. *The Gloomy Region--Erebus.*
4. *The Region of Torments—Tartarus.*
5. *The Region of Bliss—Elysium.*

1. The Previous Region. This part, the suburbs of the realms of death, Virgil has peopled with two

---

[1] "Ovid. Met." b. 4.

sorts of ideal beings. First with those which make the real misery of mankind upon Earth; such as War, Discord, Labour, Grief, Cares, Distempers, and Old age: and secondly with fancied terrors, and all the most frightful creatures of our own imagination; such as Gorgons, Harpies, Chimeras, and the like.

2. The next is the Water which all the departed were supposed to pass, to enter into the other world. This was called Styx, or the hateful passage. The imaginary personages of this division, are the souls of the departed who are either passing over, or suing for a passage; and the master of the vessel, who carries them over, one freight after another, according to his will and pleasure.

3. The third division begins immediately with the bank on the other side of the river, and was supposed to extend a great way in. It is subdivided again into several particular districts. The first seems to be the receptacle for infants. There is the limbo, for all such as have been put to death without a cause. Next is the place for those who have put a period to their own lives: a melancholy region, and situated among the marshes, made by the overflowing of the hateful river. After this are the fields of mourning, full of dark woods and groves, and inhabited by those who died for love. Last of all, spreads an open champaign country, allotted for the souls of departed warriors. The name of this whole

division is Erebus. The several districts of this division seem to be disposed all in a line, one after the other; but after this the great line or road divides into two, of which the right-hand road leads to Elysium, or the place of the blest; and the left-hand road to Tartarus, or the place of the tormented.

4. The fourth general division of the subterranean world is this Tartarus, or the place of torments. There is a city in it and a prince to preside over it. Within the city is a vast deep pit in which the tortures are supposed to be performed. In this horrid part Virgil places two sorts of souls; first, such as have shown their impiety and rebellion towards the gods; and secondly, such as have been vile or mischievous among men. Those more particularly of the latter, who hated their brethren, used their parents ill, or cheated their dependants, who made no use of their riches, who committed incest or disturbed the marriage union of others, those who were rebellious subjects, or knavish servants, who were despisers of justice and betrayers of their country, and who made and unmade laws not for the good of the public, but only to get money themselves. All these, and the despisers of the gods, Virgil places in this most horrid division of the subterranean world, and in the vast abyss which was the most horrible part of that division.

5. The fifth division is that of Elysium, or the place

of the blest. Here Virgil places those who died for their country, those of pure lives, truly inspired poets, the inventors of arts, and all who have done good to mankind. He does not speak of any particular districts for these, but supposes that they have the liberty of going where they please in that delightful region, and conversing with whom they please. He only mentions one vale towards the end of it as appropriated to any particular use, and this is the vale of Lethe, or forgetfulness; in the river of which many of the ancient philosophers supposed the souls which had passed through some periods of their trial, would be immersed as a preliminary to being put into new bodies, to fill up the remainder of their probation in our upper world. In each of these three divisions on the other side of the river Styx was a prince or judge: Minos for the regions of Erebus; Rhadamanthus for Tartarus, and Eacus for Elysium. Pluto and Proserpine had their palace at the entrance of the road to the Elysian fields, and presided as sovereigns over the whole subterranean world.[1]

Whilst this very elaborate system of future existence was being evolved by the philosophers and poets of Greece and Rome, the Sheol of the Hebrews, under the influence of Babylonian and Persian

---

[1] Virgil's " Æneid."

contact, was developing new energies and characteristics.   The Hebrews had gone into captivity with
a belief in their shadowy Sheol, the abode of shades.
Whilst Daniel by his life, and Ezekiel by his life and
writings, were protesting against the polytheistic
systems with which they were coming in contact,
they were familiarizing their fellow-countrymen with
the "beasts" and "living creatures" and all the
other imagery of the denounced creeds : and while
Ezekiel was inveighing against the form of beasts
pourtrayed upon the temple walls, he was indelibly
engraving on their minds the imagery of Babylonian
mythology, imagery which survived in full force into
Christian times, and formed the staple of the Apocalyptic vision of St. John, and an inexhaustible supply
of allegories for the pious Christians of the present day
to interpret.   But another and a greater influence
was at work.   The captive Hebrews came face to
face with the Persian theology, a pure worship of
fire ; so much akin to their own traditional worship
of Jehovah, who had manifested Himself in fire, and
who dwelt in the light that no man could approach
unto.   Nothing was so calculated as this to blot out
the lingering remnants of the gross Canaanitish rites,
which had clung like a fœtid mantle round the ideal
of their faith.   The Jews passed through their fiery
affliction of captivity, and the fiery influence of the
Zend religion, and they returned to their native land

chastened and purified. With revised ideas of the
Deity, they had imbibed revised ideas of the after
life; the souls of men, after death, no longer passed
a shadowy negative existence in a dark and silent
underworld, where few but degraded gods could
expect notice, even sufficient for punishment. But
there was a decisive judgment for all with results
trenchantly distinct; for the souls of the righteous,
a gradual and blissful reviving into new life, as stage
by stage they realize new joys until they reach
Eternal light, and are welcomed out of the corruptible
world into the imperishable life of spotless purity.
The souls of the wicked sink lower and lower, through
ever increasing stages of corruption and impurity,
until they sink into final despair. It is true that
hosts of angels and demons troop into the system,
obscuring, materializing, and degrading much that is
otherwise refined and noble in the Persian creed, but
such incrustations were and are the common inheritance of many systems, and although they obscure
they do not destroy the main distinctive features.

The outcome of all this was a belief in a Hades for
all, a Purgatory for most, and a Gehenna of fire for
a few of the eminently wicked. The Rabbins in the
Talmud revel in fanciful descriptions of the locality,
and the nature and incidents of this nether world;
but these views have been summed up as follows:—
" Ordinary transgressors of Israel, whose merits pre-

ponderate, though they descend into hell, do not feel the effects of the flames, and rise at once. Some who sin with their bodies, such as those who put their neighbours to shame publicly and who neglect the phylacteries, &c., are annihilated after twelve months' endurance of hell-fire. Adulterers, though they sin with their bodies, ascend to happiness at the end of the same period. Christians, informers, and those who systematically despise the words of the Rabbis, are consigned to eternal punishment. Of course, all may escape punishment altogether by repentance in this life."[1]

The rigid adherence of the Rabbis to their canonical texts, on which alone they allow themselves to found any statement, produces confusion in the descriptions of Hell which they attempt, for the simple reason that those texts, not dealing with such a hell, contain no description of it at all. Such, however, was the general idea entertained respecting this phase of the after life at the commencement of the Christian Era, when the missionaries of the new creed came into contact with the philosophical realization of the Hades of Greek and Latin mythologies. How far the elaborate Egyptian system of the judgment, with rewards and punishments, · directly or indirectly influenced the Jewish

---

[1] Hershon, " Talmud," 100 ; and see Matt. iii. 11 ; Mark ix. 49.

mind, it is difficult to say ; but there are certainly allusions in the Gospel narratives which are so strikingly similar to some points in the Egyptian Ritual of the Dead, as to favour the view that such influence had been brought to bear.

We have now reached a point in the evolution of Hades, where we can without difficulty recognize in the Amenti of Egypt, the Sheol and Gehenna of the Jews, and the Orcus of Virgil, all the elements of the Hell of the Christian fathers, the medieval monks, the puritans, and of the Christian religion generally. Indeed, the Hells of the Korān and of many other creeds are easily seen to be merely offshoots from the same original stock, and do not vary materially amongst themselves. The Scandinavian Valhalla, with its Purgatory, Niflheim, and its everlasting Tartarus, Nāstrond, are only variants of the same idea, where ice and howling winds however have a larger share in the economy of punishment, as representing to the hardy Norseman a greater ideal of misery than a glowing crackling fire would do.

As age after age has rolled on, as the visible world has changed, as culture has advanced, and moral and religious sanctions have been developed, the invisible world has likewise changed, the realm of " the great majority " has changed, and so have the rulers of that realm.

At first through a haze of darkness Mul-ge and Nin-ge, the shrouding spirits of the Accadian Hades

and spirits of the earth, are dimly seen commissioning
Namtar ("the fixer of Destiny"),—the plague
demon,—and other such emissaries, to collect souls
for the dread abode of death, which has little else
but negation as its characteristic.

The Sheol of the Hebrews was still less definite,
for there is no trace either of a special god, or,
which would perhaps be more orthodox, of a
presiding angel of the realms of death. Sheol was
indeed directly under the eye of Jehovah, for Sheol
and destruction are naked before Him;[1] and being
omnipresent, He is also in Sheol.[2] Sheol was too
silent,[3] its inhabitants unmurmuring like sheep,[4] too
unstrung, either to work,[5] or to praise;[6] or to require
much governing: it has gates[7] and bars,[8] and they
constitute a power sufficient for it to be likened
to jealousy in its cruelty.[9] From the antithetical
form of this simile it is to be inferred that fire was
no part of the ideal of the Hebrew Sheol: "Love is
strong as death: the coals thereof are coals of fire,
which hath a most vehement flame, many waters cannot quench love, neither can the floods drown it:
jealousy is cruel as the grave" (Sheol). Finally, Jehovah alone "bringeth down to Sheol and bringeth up."[10]

---

[1] Job xxvi. 6; Prov. xv. 11.   [2] Ps. cxxxix. 8.
[3] Ps. xxxi. 17.   [4] Ps. xlix. 14.   [5] Eccl. ix. 10.
[6] Ps. vi. 5.   [7] Is. xxxviii. 10.   [8] Job xvii. 16.
[9] Song of Solomon, viii. 6.   [10] 1 Sam. ii. 6.

The queen of the Assyrian Hades, Allat, the "queen of the divining rod," the spell-binder, is a true monarch fitted for the work of relentless vengeance, withering the condemned with curses, revelling in the exercise of her sway, and smiting her breast and biting her thumb when thwarted and overmastered by superior power. In passing, it may be remarked that Istar, the account of whose descent into Hades throws such light upon the subject, was the goddess of love and fruitfulness, and that Allat (like her Greek successor Persephone) was the goddess of death and barrenness; that a natural antagonism was likely to exist between them: and that when the waters of life had to be administered, the emblems of reproductive nature and the spirits of the earth,— the old ideal of fruitfulness,—were brought into requisition; not willingly, but by outside and superior authority; by Hea, the god of wisdom, who, by the ministration of his messenger or angel Marduk could alone annul the spells of Hades, and bring the dead to life again. The Greek Hermes,—the Latin Mercury,—who was the same as Marduk or Merodach, and who like him was the messenger of the gods, carried a magic staff or rod given to him by Phœbus, and had the power of raising the dead.

In the Greek Hades a further development takes place: Hades, brother of Zeus the god of heaven, has permanently taken up his abode in the realms of doom, wedded to his childless queen Persephone, sombrely and silently ruling the vast empire of the dead. They are at times represented as receiving the shades, as they arrive conducted by Hermes the psychopompos; but, in the Odyssey, they do not seem to judge the dead, but to leave that to their vicegerents, of whom Minos is especially named, in a passage already quoted, as placed on a throne, waving a mace of burnished gold, hearing and judging the spectres, rolling the fatal lots, absolving the just and dooming the guilty.[1]

The element of divination is still present, Allat had her divining rod; Minos has his mace of gold, and determines the fate of each soul by lot.

Hades himself was of exemplary justice, and was at one time so concerned at impediments which he found in the way of impartial judgment, that at his earnest solicitation, he obtained an amendment of the code of laws regulating the trial of the dead, which was carried out by the three judges, Minos, Rhadamanthus and Eacus.[2]

Osiris was also a permanent resident in Amenti, the Egyptian Hades, where, as above described, he sat in the Hall of the two Truths, and with the assistance of his forty-two assessors, and on the presen-

---

[1] " Odyssey," b. 11.   [2] Plato, Gorgias.

tation of Horus, his son, the Egyptian psychopompos, judged the souls of the dead, and awarded them their destiny. It is curious to trace how this idea of Osiris, as the judge, was imported into the Greek religion, and became incorporated in their system. Rā and Osiris were identical, both the Sun, the one the orb of day, the other the same orb as it passed at night through the under world : Osiris was then Rā in Amenti :—Ra-t-Amenti—whom the Greeks named Rhadamanthus. Another personification of the Sun became invested with the character of the judge of the dead : Dianysus, as the Sun, was the god of the Arabians ; according to Plutarch, Dianysus and Osiris were identical ; and according to Heraclitus, Dianysus and Hades were the same : it is probable that the name Dianysus was derived from the Assyrian words *Daian-nisi* or Dian-nisi, which means " the judge of men ;" moreover, Dionysos was the Greek Bacchus, the god of the fruitful vine, and of the rising sap of vegetation, and thus a deity of earth's productive nature.

The Roman mythology repeated that of Greece in a revised and enlarged form, and we find not only Pluto, and Proserpine, the latter the childless daughter of fruitful Ceres, and the three judges ; but we recognize Rhadamanthus,— the quondam Ra-t-Amenti, the supreme deity, the sun,—as judge of the dead, specially told off to inflict the torments of Tartarus upon rebellious gods and incorrigible men :—

> These are the realms of unrelenting fate,
> And awful Rhadamanthus rules the state.
> He hears and judges each committed crime ;
> Inquires into the manner, place and time :
> The conscious wretch must all his acts reveal;
> Loth to confess, unable to conceal ;
> From the first moment of his vital breath,
> To his last hour of unrepenting death.
>
> Had I a hundred mouths, a hundred tongues,
> And threats of brass, inspired with iron lungs,
> I could not half those horrid crimes repeat,
> Nor half the punishments those crimes have met.[1]

From the judge and inflicter of punishment for sins, in a Tartarus of fire, to the medieval or Moslem devil, who receives the wicked soul into hell fire, with the appliances of whips of flame, red hot pincers, vipers, vultures, poison and filth, there is but a step, and we can understand how this latter development followed upon that which had been building up for untold ages.

True to their original conceptions, the Jews did not create a monarch of their Gehenna, nor did the early Christians really do so : the Epistles of Peter and Jude and the Apocalypse show that Gehenna, the

---

[1] Virgil, " Æneid," Bk. 6.

bottomless pit, and the lake that burns with fire and brimstone, were prepared for the Devil and his angels; and that Satan, the Devil, that old serpent, classed with all the irretrievable wicked of the earth, were to be cast into it, not as a hierarchy with varying positions and powers, but in one common destruction. Asmodeus was the Rabbinic prince of the demons; Beelzebub was the gospel prince of the devils; and Satan, the accusing angel of the old system, was gradually growing into power, but there was no god of Hades, or of Tartaros, such as the Greeks and Romans described. The nearest approach to the expression is in the Apocalypse, where Abaddon, or Apollyon, as the personification of destruction, issuing from the bottomless pit in the form of locusts, is described as their king and the angel of the bottomless pit.

In other religions there were also judges of the dead, such as Yama, the Hindu god of hell and justice, one of many types of a first ancestor, ruling the souls of his descendants in the land of shades; and who is probably identical with Yami, the Vedic spirit of darkness, Yima, the Iranian king of paradise, O Yama, the Japanese chief of the demons, and Amma, the Sintoo god of hell. Many religions recognize death, destruction, and other abstract ideas as personified in a monarch of Hell; such as the Hindu Kali, destruction, the Gothic Kalja, the black one, and Hel or Hela, the Scandinavian goddess of death. But all these personified abstractions came too late into the Christian system to influence the evolution of the Christian ideal of the monarch of hell, the modern Satan.

With man's first belief in a future state, came his first idea of Hades,—invisible and eternal,—the abode of all the dead, both good and bad. The invisible gods fought amongst themselves, the conquerors monopolized the realms of bliss, and put the conquered under durance vile. The disembodied souls of men lived on, but practically unconscious and unnoticed, re-embodiment alone revived them. A few distinguished by great deeds or great impiety, rose to the rank of demigods, and were favoured with a god-like life of bliss or woe. As by degrees, men convinced themselves that they were equal to the gods, they claimed their privilege of conscious life, and a share of heaven and hell. Hades then required judges, executioners and varied regions of bliss and woe. The judges grew in grimness, the executioners in terror, until fear invested many of the judges and all the executioners with such hateful attributes, that their merger into the personality of the Devil,—man's adversary and accuser,—was the result. Hatred led to revenge, and this concentrated judge and executioner has been himself at last linked with his prisoners, and condemned to everlasting punishment.

M

FIRE.

THE element of fire has in all ages appealed to the
deepest feelings of mankind. This is not surprising:
the most prosaic utilitarian is bound to admit its
value in daily life: the least poetical observer of
Nature can hardly stand unmoved in the presence of
the sun in all the golden glory of his setting: and
the lightning flash, the rocking earthquake, and the
volcanic outburst, must arrest the attention of the
most indifferent. The brute creation is equally im-
pressed by these developments of fire: animals court
and enjoy its mild warmth: the rising sun awakens
the woods to melodious joy, and makes them teem
with life: the storm and earthquake paralyze all
Nature into deadly silence with overwhelming dread:
the lava stream and prairie fire make hungry beasts

of prey forget their savage instincts, in the panic-
stricken struggle to escape : and even the encamp-
ment fire suffices to keep off the prowling wolf by a
kind of fascination.

It is difficult to realize what the world was without fire ; or rather, without the utilization of fire ;
for man must always have had some experience of
fire as a physical fact; the lightning, the burning
mountain, the sparks from the flints which the river-
drift man chipped for his weapons and tools, must
have made the phenomena of fire familiar ; but until
man had learnt how to use and perpetuate fire and
artificial light, what a strange existence must his
have been! No cooked food, no metals, no bricks ;
nothing to scare away the midnight foe, to counteract
miasmatic damps, or biting frosts : nothing to relieve
the long dark nights of winter.   Who could be sur-
prised at man, under such circumstances, looking up
to heaven, and saluting the sun as his best friend ;
and regarding the rest of the heavenly host as the
sun's attendants ; or at his mourning and desponding
as the days grew shorter and shorter ; and rejoicing at
the birth of the new year, when the crisis of winter
was passed and the dark dread nights became less
and less wearisome and chill ?

We can well imagine that before the days of fire
and artificial light, men " lived as infants, ...
who, seeing, saw in vain, hearing they heard not.

But like to the form of dreams, for a long time they used to huddle together all things at random, and nought knew they about brick-built and sun-ward houses, nor carpentry; but they dwelt in the excavated earth, like tiny emmets in the sunless depths of caverns."[1]

In our own age we are just beginning to realize some of the benefits which can be derived by bringing under control one of the great forces of Nature, electricity, which for countless ages had only been recognized as the manifestation of a wrathful deity: now, like the spirit in Faust within the pentagram, confined within the narrow limits of a gutta-percha film, and a most obedient servant. How much greater must have been the stride which marked the transition from ignorance to knowledge of the art of creating and preserving fire, and its use for human wants; how arts of every kind became possible, and were developed one by one, each upon the foundation of its predecessor, until the dreaded demon, fire, once only known as the agent of destruction, became the slave of man.

How fire was first created and subdued for the use of man, cannot now be shown; many theories are equally possible; but one method of procuring it has received such marked honour, and has come down to

---

[1] Æsch. Prom. 446.

us so wonderfully imbedded in the earliest stratum of history, as to demand especial notice. "Pramantha" is the Sanskrit name for the old fire-drill, which is the earliest known instrument for procuring fire. It consisted of a stick like an arrow shaft, cut to a blunt point, which was twirled .between the hands, with such speed and pressure as to bore a hole in an under piece of wood, till the charred dust made by the boring took fire.[1] "Prometheus" is the Titan of the Aryan mythology, who stole fire from heaven, concealed in a fennel stick, and gave it to men, who have ever since procured fire by using a "pramantha," a fire drill, often made with a fennel stick. The wrath of Zeus at "creatures of a day possessing bright fire," is difficult to understand, unless there be an explanation in the jealousy of some dominant race, at the acquisition of fire by a class of down-trodden slaves : it has been suggested that there may be some relation between this acquisition of fire, and that of the fruit of the tree of knowledge in the garden of Eden, which had been forbidden to mortals; but which, when seized and appropriated, made them as Jehovah-Elohim in their power of knowledge : the mysterious association of Jehovah with fire lends some colour to this supposition.

In reference to this last suggestion, the oldest

---

[1] Tylor's Anthro. 261.

myths in the world have references to the invention
of fire, and to the waters of life, which are very
remarkable. The idea that fire was forbidden fruit
is found in the Vêdas, and was passed on in modified
forms to the Greeks, the Romans, and the Slavs ;
it is also found amongst the Iranians and the Hindus.
The basis of these myths,—which are not found complete except under their oldest forms,—represents the
universe as an immense tree, of which the roots
surround the earth, and the branches form the vault
of heaven. The fruit of this tree is fire, indis-
pensable to the existence of man, and material
symbol of intelligence ; its leaves distil the water of
life. The gods have reserved to themselves the
possession of fire, which descends at times upon the
earth in lightning, but men ought not to produce it
themselves. He who, like the Prometheus of the
Greeks, discovers the method which enables him to
light it artificially, and to communicate it to other
men, is impious, and has stolen the forbidden fruit
of the holy tree. He is cursed, and the wrath of
the gods pursues him and his race.[1]

Prometheus, the demi-god, who snatched the sacred
fire and gave it over to men, was condemned to be
chained alive to a rock in the remote Caucasus
mountains, and to submit, while every day a vulture

---

[1] Lenormant, " Origines d'Histoire," 96–7.

came to gnaw away his liver, which daily grew afresh. But Prometheus was proud; he had alone saved the human race from the destruction which all the other gods had planned; and those that he had ransomed he took in hand to educate: having brought them fire and light, he proceeded to teach them numbers, memory, agriculture, sailing, medicine, divination, augury and metal-working; and in one brief sentence he could truly boast " All arts among the human race are from Prometheus."[1]

We must still bear in mind the animistic faith of primeval man, and that it was in the nature of such belief to realize the spirit as resembling the tangible appearance. As visible fire was in itself almost spiritual in its nature,—fitful and formless;—so the spirits of fire were more ethereal than the spirits of inert and material bodies. All spirits, too, were hungry beings, and, as the offerings to fire were visibly consumed by the spirit under the very eye of the votary, so confidence in the propitiation of these powerful spirits was the more surely felt as the result. The sun in the heavens and the fire on the earth had points in common, light and warmth, which had had little existence away from the sun before the invention of fire. The light and warmth produced by art were therefore part of the solar

---

[1] Æsch. Prom.

light and warmth, which had been brought down from heaven to earth, concealed in the fennel stick from which they were afterwards procured. The worship of fire was a natural development of that of the sun, and from the absence of bodily form, and the comparative abstractness of the ideal, fire-worship was certainly of a purer type than were most other religions.

Fire once acquired and its value understood, its preservation and accessibility became a matter of cardinal importance : hence regulations of the earliest date for maintaining perpetual fire in a temple or other public building. Every tribe had its central fire, from which all could draw, and so had every town and village. The sacredness of this perpetual fire was an article of faith ; it was the direct gift of heaven, a part of heaven itself. In Rome the Vestal virgins had to watch the fire untiringly, and if perchance this fire went out, not only was there a most severe penalty for the impious neglect, but all tribunals, all authority, all public and private business were stopped, until the celestial fire was re-kindled. The connection between heaven and earth had been broken, and had to be restored : and this had to be brought about, either by Jove's lightning flash, or by new fire obtained by the priests rubbing two pieces of wood together, or by using a concave mirror in the sunshine. The sacred fire radiated through the whole community; the altar with its fire travelled with every army, and to every colony, and into every family and hut. The fire temple was the place for every solemn act, the reception of ambassadors, the discussion of public policy, the transaction of business, and the award of justice. The domestic hearth became the rallying point of the family, the centre of parental influence, where truth and purity should reign; for the deity was there, casting light upon and taking note of all that passed. The public maintenance of sacred fire was not only an institution of the ancient Greeks and Romans, but also of the Jews, Chaldeans, Tartars, Chinese, and other Mongolian tribes; Egyptians, Ethiopians and Japanese; Mexicans, Peruvians, and other tribes of the new world; so that it may be fairly styled universal in ancient times. The lamps kept burning in synagogues, and in the Byzantine and Catholic churches, are probably a survival of the ancient, sacred, and perpetual fire. The ceremonies amongst the Aztecs attending the extinction of the old fire at the end of every cycle of fifty-two years, and the creation of the new fire, and with it the renovation of all domestic associations, are very graphically described in Prescott's "History of the Conquest of Mexico."[1] The Aztecs

Vol. i. p. 69.

were very much in earnest, and gave in practice full evidence of their earnestness in relation to this new fire.

The Fire-god took many forms, and his worship being so widespread, we cannot wonder at finding the ideal considerably varied. In the Aryan religion Agni was the fire-god, and it has been pointed out that the name of Agni is the first word of the first hymn of the Rig-Veda, one of the most venerable (and perhaps even the oldest) of the sacred records in the world, "Agni I entreat, divine appointed priest of sacrifice!"[1]

The Accadians and Assyrians had an equal veneration for their fire-god :—

> O Fire, great lord, who art the most exalted in the world,
> Noble son of heaven, thou art the most exalted in the world.
> O Fire, with thy bright flame
> In the dark house thou dost cause light.
> Of all things that can be named, thou dost form the fabric!
> Of bronze and of lead thou art the melter!
> Of silver and of gold thou art the refiner,
> Of the wicked man in the night-time, thou dost repel the assault!
> But the man who serves his god, thou wilt give him light for his actions.[2]

It is to be noted that the name of Izdhubar, the hero of the great Accadian epic, signifies, " a mass of

---

[1] Tylor's " Prim. Cul." ii. 281.
[2] " Records of the Past," iii. 137.

fire," showing that he was identical with the Accadian fire-god, who in this case was also the sun. Mr.
George Smith in his Chaldean Genesis identifies
him with the Biblical Nimrod, "the mighty hunter
before the Lord :"[1] and it is certain that he belongs
to the class of heroes, whose exploits, woven on to
the framework of a zodiac, with twelve signs, have
given us, not only the Accadian epic, but also that
of the Odyssey, and the labours of Hercules, and
many other compilations of the world's most ancient
traditions.[2]

The essential principle of fire was supposed to
pervade all Nature, and spirits were conceived as
beings of fire : the good or celestial spirits,—the
devas, the shining ones, the "angels bright and fair,"—
of refulgent whiteness. The vision at the opening of
the Apocalypse is described thus :—" His head and
his hairs were white like wool, as white as snow ;
and his eyes were like a flame of fire : and his feet
like unto fine brass, as if they burned in a furnace ;
. . . . . and his countenance was as the sun shineth
in its strength."[3] The seven Spirits of God were
also seen as seven lamps of fire, burning before His
throne :[4] He, too, dwelleth in the light that no
man can approach unto : and the Spirit, when He

---

[1] Smith's "Genesis," Sayce, 176. [2] *Ib.* 177.
[3] Rev. i. 13–16. [4] Rev. v. 5.

descended upon the Apostles on the day of Pentecost, did so in the form of tongues of fire.

The spirits of earth, living in the cavernous depths, are not of this refulgent type ; they are still of fire, but heavier, duller, more lurid : they are accordingly composed of red fire, and not white. Thor, the Scandinavian god of fire, of agriculture, and of the domestic hearth, was a *red*-haired and *red*-bearded man ; and fire-gods generally were *red* or had *red* beards : the history of Esau, the Hebrew Satyr, is tinged with *red* throughout ;[1] the heifer which was to be the whole burnt offering in the Mosaic ritual was to be *red*, and its *red* hide was specially directed to be burnt ;[2] a South Pacific legend makes a *red* pigeon the means of procuring fire from the sub-terranean fire-demon ; the dwarfs and fairies, the successors of the ancient fire-worshippers, generally have *red* caps, which are their means of preserving the spiritual attribute of invisibility ; the kobolds, or goblins, are fiery imps who sport *red* jackets ;[3] and finally Mephistopheles would certainly not be recognized in any but a scarlet garb :—

> Here as a youth of high degree,
> I come in gold lac'd *scarlet* vest.[4]

Intimately associated with the idea of supernatural

---

[1] See p. 224.   [2] Numbers xix. 2.
[3] Keightley's " Fairy Mythology," 253.   [4] "Faust," 1183–84.

beings of fire, would be the celestial bodies, far beyond the reach of mortal man, but always living and moving, some influencing in fact the economy of Nature, and the others believed to influence it, if not in an apparent, yet in some occult mode. The wide-spread worship of the sun has been already referred to, and will not be further examined here : we have seen how Bel was the sun, became identified with Baal, and degenerated into Beelzebub, the prince of the devils. A similiar track was followed by Duzi, or Damuzi, the sun that has set, who became known in Biblical times as Tammuz, and to the Sabeans as Taus, and who is now worshipped under the name of Taous, in the form of a peacock, by the Yzedis, the so-called devil worshippers of Mesopotamia. The Syrian Tammuz and the Greek Adonis (Syrian Adonai, *Lord*) have long been recognized as identical ; and Apollo, Helios, Phœbus and Dianysos have all in turn been sun-gods, and their identity and attri-butes have been overlapped and interchanged, past unravelling. The Phœnix, periodically dying and reviving, and the mythical Rokh of Arabian mytho-logy, no doubt owe their origin to a common source with the deified peacock Taous.

We have seen how Izdhubar-Nimrod, the mighty hunter,. and Hercules, and the host of other heroes and demigods, who labour through a cycle of varied toils and journeys, timed to the zodiacal signs, like the sun, have probably a common origin. The events of ages have brought these doughty heroes down through Odin, and the wild huntsman of German folk-lore,—a demon who hunts with a pack of hell-hounds,—to the blue-fire fiend of English legends, Herne the hunter.

All these were personifications of the sun, the powerful focus of celestial fire, who for ages reigned as the supreme god of the universe; whose rising through the golden portals of the eastern sky could furnish a figure in sublimest language of the coming of Jehovah Himself: " Lift up your heads, O ye gates; and be ye lift up, ye everlasting doors; and the king of glory shall come in. . . . . the Lord strong and mighty, the Lord mighty in battle."[1] And even, the ideal bridegroom of mythology, Tammuz-Adonis, as the sun in the heavens, is made to declare the glory of Jehovah to every nation throughout the world; for he is " As a bridegroom coming out of his chamber and rejoiceth as a strong man to run a race. His going forth is from the end of the heaven, and his circuit unto the ends of it : and there is nothing hid from the heat thereof."[2]   Nothing was hid from the heat of the sun, and his heat was not lost when he passed through the caverns under the earth, between his setting and his rising again; and subterranean

---

[1] Ps. xxiv. 7, 8.   [2] Ps. xix. 1–7.

heat and fire, and fructifying warmth were associated with, if not produced by, the sun in the course of his circuits of perpetual activity : realizing the figure of the husband,—the bridegroom of the earth.

Another form of fire could not fail to impress man with the greatest awe. Thinking man might be brought to conclude that the sun could not be a god, or he would not pursue his monotonous journey like a mill-horse, but would show some signs of independent action. But this idea would not attach to the lightning and thunder. The storm-clouds gathering over some devoted spot, according to no apparent law of Nature, flashing down their lightning at unequal intervals, striking hither and thither with destructive force, and roaring all the time with a stupendous voice, which drowns all other sounds besides, filling the mind with a profound sense of human impotence ; became the ideal of gods of power and independent action. Dyaus-pitar (heaven father), the Aryan god of the expanse of heaven, Indra, his Hindu counterpart, Zeus, the Greek divinity, and Jupiter, the Latin god of heaven, all wielded the thunderbolt, and executed speedy judgment on any who became the object of divine wrath.

The discovery of fire had been an epoch in the history of man, the use of metals was hardly less important as an acquisition. Tubal-cain, whether this name be that of an individual or of a tribe, who

introduced the art of working brass (bronze) and
iron, brought about a complete revolution in the
world. The tribes who only knew of arms and tools
of chipped stone, bone or wood were soon mastered
by the metal-working races; and although a magic
glamour enveloped the people of the old stone age,
yet the dread of iron, and its power to overcome the
magic influences, have survived in mythology and
folk-lore to a most remarkable extent. In the oldest
legends of all, a wooden rod or wand was the instrument for overcoming spells and sorcery. Izdhubar,
when he engaged in his perilous journey to the
land of the departed, provided himself with a wand
or spear of special efficiency to resist obstructive
powers; the rod of Moses was made the visible
instrument of his power, and was afterwards preserved with reverential care; the thyrsos of Mercury,
and similar emblems borne by many other gods in
the hand; the divining rod of conjurors and the wand
of the fairy; perhaps even the sceptre of the king,
and the baton of the field-marshal, are all insignia
of power, relics inherited from remotest time, before
metal arms ruled the world by force. But iron was
stronger still; Ulysses held the shades at bay with
his brandished falchion : the oriental jinn are in such
deadly terror of iron, that its very name is a charm
against them : and in European folk-lore iron drives

---

[1] Keightley's " Fairy Mythology," 26.

away fairies and elves, and destroys their power ; iron instruments are equally potent against witches, and especially have iron horse-shoes been chosen for this purpose, as half the stable doors in England testify.[1]

Stratum after stratum of the human race has become buried or absorbed by succeeding waves, and the little people of the stone age, or rather the distinctive generations of them, died out, and only left behind them relics, memories and superstitions. Succeeding generations acquired the practice of the art of metal-working, and brought it to the highest perfection. According to the Mosaic account, Tubal-cain was the first instructor of every artificer in brass and iron : among the Greeks Hephaestos was the god of subterranean fire, working in a smoky smithy down in the heart of burning mountains, and forging arms and armour, and other works in metal of surpassing beauty and temper : the Latins had their Vulcan (whose name some have sought to identify with that of Tubal-cain), whose occupations were similar to those of Hephaestos, and who moreover forged the thunderbolts for Jove, his father : Loki, the Scandinavian Vulcan, was more lively and mischievous than the Latin god, but he shared with him his skill in metal-working of unrivalled strength and beauty. These

---

[1] Tylor's "Prim. Cul." 140. Keightley's "Fairy Mythology," 26, 148, 413, 488.

gods of the internal fire were aided by Kyklops, and other like attendants : and these grim metal-workers crop up in fairy mythology as the black dwarfs, who "are horridly ugly, with weeping eyes, like blacksmiths and colliers. They are most expert workmen, especially in steel, to which they can give a degree at once of hardness and flexibility which no human smith can imitate ; for the swords they make will bend like rushes, and are as hard as diamonds. In old times arms and armour made by them were in great request; shirts of mail manufactured by them were as fine as cobwebs, and yet no bullet would penetrate them, and no helm or corslet could resist the swords they fashioned ; but all these things are now gone out of use."[1]

It requires very little speculation to understand how these gods of the internal fire, invested with repulsive attributes, became associated in the mind with the presiding deities of the subterranean abodes of the dead, and why they should be relegated to that part of Hades where the fires of Tartaros were placed. Hephaestos, Vulcan and Loki, each lame from some deformity of foot, in time joined natures with the pans and satyrs of the upper world; the lame sooty blacksmith donned their goatlike extremities of cloven hoofs, tail and horns ; and the

---

[1] Keightley's " Fairy Mythology," 176.

black dwarfs became the uncouth ministers of this sooty, black, foul fiend. If ever mortal man accepted the services of these cunning metal-workers, it was for some sinister purpose, and at a fearful price—no less than that of the soul itself, bartered away in a contract of red blood, the emblem of life and the colour of fire.

Fire in another aspect is distinctively the consuming element; and this phase of its power must always have been that most forcibly realized by man. When fire was the supreme god, and souls and spirits were like flames, death was the extinction of the "vital spark;" the body dropped lifeless and inert; left to itself its fate would be "to lie in cold obstruction and to rot."[1] Then was the time when pious sons would raise the funeral pyre, and by consuming the material body of the dead, would send that body to the land of shades, to be there reunited to the ethereal soul, and so secure a passage over the dread waters of the Styx; to a place where some hope, however vague, of a kind of future life, and even of happiness, was possible. Those who were shipwrecked and whose carcasses were swallowed by the deep, or lay unburied on the shore; those who left no descendants willing to light up the funeral fires, or compose the bones in graves with funeral dues, were doomed to

---

[1] "Measure for Measure," act iii. sc. I.

double disembodiment; they not only lost their bodies, but also that something between a body and a soul, which was set free and despatched to the nether regions by the burning of the body, or the performance of other regular sepulchral rites; and this dire condition they were destined to endure for a hundred years, or until the funeral rites were performed.

> The ghosts rejected are th' unhappy crew
> Depriv'd of sepulchres, and fun'ral due.
> The boatman Charon; those the bury'd host,
> He ferries over to the farther coast.
> Nor dares his transport vessel cross the waves
> With such whose bones are not compos'd in graves.
> A hundred years they wander on the shore,
> At length their penance done, are wafted o'er.[1]

The idea is related to that which gave rise amongst so many races to the destruction by fire or by dedication in the tomb, of food, clothing, arms, horses, slaves and wives, to serve the great departed in the land of shades : of which the Hindu suttee was one development. But associated with this was the realization of the diety as a hungry demon, the Devourer *par excellence.* Loki, the Scandinavian god of subterranean fire, was a great devourer, and was ready to challenge any other being, god or man, to an eating match, and he was met and beaten by Logi,

---

[1] Dryden's " Virgil's ' Æneid,'" b. 6.

FIRE

the Scandinavian god of devouring fire,[1] such it is
assumed, as a prairie fire or forest fire. The older
gods of the Greeks and Romans, Kronos and Saturn,
were devouring gods who were not only pleased with
perpetual sacrifices, but went to the length of devouring their own offspring; and even Zeus himself, of the
later race of gods, once gave way to this devouring
propensity when he swallowed his wife, Metis. Again
Moloch, the great Phœnician god, was generally
identified by the Greeks with Kronos, and he was
essentially a hungry and blood-thirsty deity.
Moloch has always been associated with fire, although
perhaps strictly not a fire-god: he was worshipped,
not only by victims being consumed in his presence,
but even by their being thrown into his belly of fire:
his image is described as of brass, hollow within, and
with a head like a calf, and outstretched arms into
which were thrown the victims, who sank down into
the fire, which was kindled in the belly. The worship
of this Phœnician god by these rites was wide-spread,
and it was so well established as to be almost ineradi-
cable, even under the strong denunciation of the
Hebrew prophets, who inveighed against the passing
of children through the fire to Moloch. This form of
human sacrifice, if indeed it ever was subdued,
smouldered on amongst the Hebrews, and again

---

[1] Mallet's "Northern Antiquities," 439.

burst forth in full vigour under the monarchy, when
Solomon and Manasseh successively set up this
worship, and sons were passed through the fire to
Moloch and to Chemosh, his Moabitish counterpart.
It is probable that the worship of Baal, the sun-god,
became in time blended with that of the devouring
deities, and that the same rites were eventually
observed in both.

We have already seen that, amongst the Hebrews,
fire held an important place in their conception of the
Deity ; and their declension to a worship of material
fire, and sacrifices to the local fire god, is quite
intelligible. In the time of Jeremiah, the prophet,
in the valley of the son of Hinnom (Ge-hinnom)
situate outside the city of Jerusalem, on the East
side, at the sun-gate ;—near which Ezekiel in his
vision saw the twenty-five men worshipping the sun,
and turning their backs on the Temple,—stood
Moloch's altar, and young children were thrown
into the cruel arms of the brazen god, to the sound of
the toph, the drum, beaten to drown the cries of the
victims, and to excite the people : from whence the
name of Tophet. This valley was to the Hebrew
prophet a place of dire abomination, and drew down
the most scathing denunciation. Josiah, the king,
defiled the valley in some way calculated to make the
place unfit for any religous service ; for, degrading as
the worship was, it was hedged round by superstitious

rules. It became thenceforth a place of burning for dead carcasses and offal ;—the type of corruption, and of the valley of death ;—and the ideal of that hell of fire, which was at once the place of retribution and of purification, realized by the later Jews.

When the Jews returned from the Babylonish captivity, they brought with them a name for Hades, Gehenna, derived from the old Accadian records, in which Gi-umuna means the foundation of " chaos,"[1] the old Hebrew Sheol. They also brought back their Persian ideal of a fiery place of retribution and purification ; and by a transition, easy to the Jews, the abominable valley of perpetual burnings, corruption, and fœtid smoke;—identified with traditions of human sacrifices, and the presence of heathen gods, now demonized ; the old Ge-hinnom—became the new Gehenna, the latter inheriting the horrible traditions of the former, both of human sacrifices by fire, and of the burning of the dead, by which those sacrifices had been superseded : in each case fire was the leading idea, and furnished the facts and figures of the Jewish Tartaros. Having localized this place of retribution, one step further placed upon the throne of that burning world, Asmodeus, the arch-demon of the impure fire, who had come back with the Jews from the land of Media.

---

[1] " Chaldean Magic," 166–170, &c.

The impure fire,—this is the real point of contact between the element of fire and the ideal devil :—the fire of passion, wrath and lust : the fire that eats into the moral being as a canker ; turning all that was sound and beautiful, into rottenness and repulsive hideousness : it is the hell which setteth on fire the whole course of Nature,[1] and incites to all kinds of lust and crime ; it is the fever which possesses erring man until "the whole head is sick, and the whole heart faint. From the sole of the foot even unto the head there is no soundness in it ; but wounds and bruises and putrefying sores :" until the " sins are as *scarlet* and *red* like *crimson.*"[2]

We have already referred to Lilith, the Rabbinic first wife of Adam, and to the probable association with her, of the tradition of moral degradation in pre-historic times. The elaboration of the idea is of comparatively late growth ; but the idea itself, as a foundation, is of far greater antiquity : by reading between the lines of the Hebrew canon, not only is it possible to see that some such object was present to the writers, but that it was one of their great desiderata, to counteract the influence of the old tradition, and to wean their readers from its dangers.

No one can read the Hebrew history, either in

---

[1] James iii. 6.   [2] Isaiah i. 5, 6, 18.

the Bible, or in the Talmudic writings, without recognizing that the besetting sin of the Hebrew race was that of carnal lust. In the Bible, we have the history of the Hebrew race, promulgated as an authentic record. It purports in its earlier chapters to give an account of the origin of all things, of man and all the nations upon earth, but the document which has come down to us, was not compiled until after the Hebrews had become a nation, and we can see that the writer kept steadily in view the separation, from the rest of the world, of the peculiar people, and the establishment of those institutions by which they were to be distinguished. The existence and history of collateral off-shoots from the Hebrew genealogical tree, are either not noticed at all, or are but barely referred to. The great desideratum of the Hebrew law-giver and his immediate successor was to prevent their followers from mixing with the Canaanitish nations, who retained the traditions of the hated past ; and the pitiless command went forth, to "save alive nothing that breatheth," so as to prevent the possibility of contamination. In the history of the nation, prominence was given to all the facts which could create abhorrence of the superseded system and its votaries.: the fall of Eve brought about by a being in the form of a serpent, the ancient object of worship ; the murder of the shepherd Abel by the

agriculturist Cain, and the curse which followed;
the curse of Ham, the progenitor of Canaan and the
Canaanites ; the destruction of the cities of the plain
where the obscenity of the old religion was especially
rampant; the declension of Baal-peor, and the
destruction by plague of 24,000 Hebrew men which
followed; all pointing the moral against the old
system of lewdness. No wonder that tradition eventually personified this old system as Lilith, a beautiful woman, and described her as endowed with
magic powers, as having been the first but cast-off
wife of Adam, and that being the jealous enemy of
Eve, she had assumed the form of a serpent,—a
seraph, or angel of light,—and had succeeded in
conquering her, and bringing her and all her
offspring to misery. This was indeed the legend of
the Rabbins, who also made Lilith, the mother
of the jinns or demons, including Asmodeus, the
Persian demon of lust, who, in course of time,
succeeded to a post of the highest rank in the
demonic hierarchy.

Purity was the ideal of the Hebrew good ; Lust
and Immorality, so closely woven into the religion
of the Canaanites, and other aboriginal and early
nations, were the great opposing principle confront-
ing this ideal, and denounced vehemently throughout
their sacred books as the great evil: the spiritual
personification of this opposing principle was the

nearest idea of a devil which they ever attained. The Hebrews themselves were a cruel, blood-thirsty race ; their system of warfare was atrocious in the extreme ; and their religious rites demanded a perpetual shedding of blood, their priests being really the butchers of the nation : but this was deemed necessary both for the suppression of a still greater evil, and as a mitigation of a still greater atrocity : the old corrupt system was the evil, and the atrocity to be mitigated was human sacrifice in its most repulsive form.

Among the Persians the fire which they associated so prominently with the spiritual beings of their religion, was at an early date separated into the two great divisions of celestial fire, and infernal fire. The former was personified as Ashavahista, the spirit of "supreme purity;" the latter as Aēshma-daēva, the spirit of the "impure fire." In the great combat between Ahura-mazda (Ormuzd) and Anrō-mainyu (Ahriman), these two spirits of fire are pitted against one another.

We have seen how the captive Jews were led by a similarity of traditions, to sympathize with the Persian religious teaching, and how, on their return from captivity, the Jewish religious system became deeply tinged, and even imbued with Persian doctrines. Amongst these doctrines was that of the hierarchy of demons or devils, with Aschmedai, the quondam Aēshma-daēva, the arch-demon of lust, as the most potent of the infernal fiends. In the apocryphal book of Tobit Aschmedai is a principal actor, who is not only burning with lust but also with jealousy, and who slays the first seven husbands of Sara, in the vain hope of securing her for himself.

The antagonism which existed from the earliest times between the Iranian, the Persian race, and the cognate race of Hindus, whose religious rites were to the last degree obscene, may have led to the accentuation of their detestation for such characters as were typified by Aschmedai; and found other developments in the belief in succubi and incubi, the spirits of impurity, who, prowling through the darkness of the night, instilled into the mind unholy thoughts, and corrupted the body with pollution. It then was and still is the practice of Hindu races, not only to permit, but to enjoin as a duty such rites in connection with religion, observed to this day in their very temples, as do not yield in impurity to the worship of Mylitta, for which Babylon has in history gained such unenviable notoriety.

Aschmedai in later writings became the more familiar Asmodeus, who furnished the industrious, tradition-weaving Rabbins with a hero, always available as the principal actor in some brand-new ancient legend, pieced together for the instruction or entertainment of the schools of learning; assemblies which these Rabbins so much enjoyed that they modelled their heaven on the same pattern.

The Rabbins did not consider Asmodeus as a spirit of unmixed evil, as the following legend will show;— Solomon was commanded to build the Temple without using iron tools; and being in perplexity how to fulfil the divine command, was advised to have recourse to a certain magical insect, called the Shamir, which had the power of cutting through the hardest stone : it was not known where the Shamir was to be found, and it was thought that the demons might disclose its whereabouts. The male and female demons were accordingly interrogated, under the persuasive influence of the rack, but without effect, for they did not know: they however, suggested that Asmodeus, "the king of the demons," might be in possession of the Shamir. Questioned as to the abode of Asmodeus, they replied that he usually resided on a certain mountain, and described the exact spot; that he ascended daily into heaven, for the purpose of attending the celestial seat of learning; and of coming down in order to be present at the sublunary debating rooms; and that on returning home he was accustomed to drink of a particular well. A messenger was accordingly despatched with a quantity of wine, and a magic chain, on which the name of God was engraved : the

water was drawn off from the well, and the wine
was substituted. The device succeeded, Asmodeus
drank deeply of the wine, was overpowered, and
chained by the magic chain, which he could not
shake off, and led away captive to Solomon. On the
journey he came in contact with a palm tree, which
was snapped by his weight. He was about to do
the same to a widow's cottage, but yielded to her
entreaties for mercy, and refrained, but in stooping
to get out of the way, he broke a bone in his leg, and
became lame. They passed a blind man and a
drunkard, who had lost their way; and he put both
of them right again; at the same time telling his
captors, that the former was known in heaven as a
perfectly righteous man, and the latter as a perfectly
wicked one. Besides these he gave other surprising
evidence of his foreknowledge with regard to persons
casually met on the road. On his arrival, he put
Solomon in the way of procuring the Shamir, and
remained in his service until the Temple was com-
pleted. During his stay he became very intimate
with Solomon, and one day, during a friendly discussion as to feats of skill, managed to shoot Solomon
away bodily to a distance of four hundred miles ;
and assuming his form and appearance, took possession of his harem. Solomon, like Ulysses, had to
find his way back home, where his identity was at
first doubted. Eventually, the personation was de-

tected, and a magic ring and chain, engraved with
the names of God, put Asmodeus to flight, and
Solomon was restored to his throne and home.[1]

It is to be observed in this legend, that Asmodeus,
the king of demons, like the Satan of Job, and the
lying spirit of Ahab's time, had access to the presence of God ; that he is not unmoved by feelings of
compassion, and that he is not thought unworthy to
be employed in the erection of the great temple of
Jehovah, which even David, the man after God's own
heart, was not allowed to build.

Asmodeus travelled through the early Christian
ages and medieval times, side by side with other
demons, endowed with various attributes of evil ;
but although from time to time he changed his form,
and was often overshadowed by darker conceptions,
he fairly held his own : and indeed the ideal Devil
always retained his lustful character.   A Mussulman
legend relates of Iblis, the Arabian Devil, that Allah
gave him for food, all things sacrificed to idols ; for
drink, wine and intoxicating liquors ; for amusement,
music, song, love, poetry and dancing ; and although
his regular home was to be ruins, tombs and unclean
places, yet he was to have liberty to curse Allah, and
was promised a progeny which should outnumber
the guardian angels in the proportion of seven to

[1] Hershon's " Genesis according to the Talmud," 188.

two ; and that, except with the faithful few, the evil should prevail.[1]

If this was the appointed lot of the Devil, we cannot wonder that shoals of men were found ready to enlist under his banners, and to enjoy " the pleasures of sin for a season," regardless of the end to which it led. The Devil thus had too many disciples among men to make him at any time absolutely unpopular, and Le Sage's lame Asmodeus, the "Devil-on-two-Sticks," is a strange mixture of philosophy, cynical wickedness, and common sense.

But another change was to come over this aggressive spirit. Children in their childhood, and rustics all their lives, might believe in a black Devil with tail and horns and cloven hoofs. But such a personality could not survive, and dropped into the limbo of vain conceits. The traditional form had disappeared, but not his works : he was as untiring, as industrious as ever : unseen, unrecognized, he threaded his way through crowded humanity, wherever thought was lightest and joy the highest : he would penetrate into the seclusion of the cloister and the cell, and whisper his temptations to the ascetic and the student. The old coarse notion of the Devil carried with it a wholesome panic dread, which, if it influenced at all, tended to repulsion.

---

[1] Conway's "Demonology," ii. 261.

But the ideal of evil, which grew more and more refined as the culture advanced with which it kept pace, was far more insidious; and grew in strength and power to influence and subjugate, as the old form disappeared, and gave place to a graceful spirit of refinement and elegance.

Mephis. The culture, too, that shapes the world, at last
Hath e'en the devil in its sphere embraced;
The northern phantom from the scene hath passed,
Tail, talons, horns, are nowhere to be traced!
As for the foot, with which I can't dispense,
'Twould injure me in company, and hence,
Like many a youthful cavalier,
False calves I now have worn for many a year.

Witch. I am beside myself with joy,
To see once more the gallant Satan here!

Mephis. Woman, no more that name employ!

Witch. But why? What mischief has it done?

Mephis. To fable it too long hath appertained;
But people from the change have nothing won,
Rid of the Evil *One*, the *evil* has remained.[1]

So spake Mephistopheles, the courtly, seeming slave, but real master. The grimy garb, the brawny arms, and rough sledge-hammer of Vulcan have given place to the "gold-laced scarlet vest, the stiff silk mantle, the gay feather, and the long pointed rapier," and well-turned limbs of the youth of high degree, into whom he has become transformed.

[1] Goethe's "Faust," 2146-55; 2156-60.

O

The material fire, and the tool of brute force, formidable, but capable of useful work, have been replaced by the moral fire, and the polished and more deadly arm, made only for the purpose of destruction.

VIII

DRAGONS AND SATYRS.

Primeval Monsters — Honesty of Mythological Traditions — Ichthyosaurus—Plesiosaurus — Atlantosaurus — Pterodactyle —Fights with Dragons—Leviathan—Facts precede Ideals— Composite Animals—Chaos—Babylonian Monsters—Scorpion Men—Æneas—Hesiodic Monsters—St. Michael—St. George and the Dragon—Dragons of Romance and Poetry—Bunyan's Apollyon — Satyrs and Pans — River-drift Man — Aborigines —Man and the Ape—Hea-bani—Hebrew Satyrs—Horns.

In examining the physical forms attributed to the Devil, it is hardly possible to avoid concluding that traditions of primeval monsters, the existence of which, at one time, cannot be doubted, are accountable for some of the most characteristic types. These monsters were by their aspect and ferocity, calculated to strike terror into all beholders ; and to fix upon their memories an indelible impression of physical evil, and of irresistible malignant power. Such experience and impressions must have been passed on from generation to generation, with that vividness and exaggeration which are born of a horrible terror. As these races of monsters gradually died out, and at last became extinct, the traditions of them became less and less capable of

verification by contemporary facts ; and those traditions would thus become more and more misunder-
stood and distorted, although still preserving their
general character and truthfulness.

In matters of religious belief, the world has exercised far more sobriety and conscientiousness than
it has credit for ; and these virtues are, as a rule,
manifested in the inverse proportion to the culture of a race or community. There is no evidence
—and in the absence of evidence it ought not to be
assumed—that at any time in the world's history,
has any individual, or body of men, deliberately set
to work to originate mythological traditions, for the
purpose of either deceiving their contemporaries, or
imposing upon posterity. Uncultured or simply
cultured man is far too much surrounded by the
unknown and the inexplicable ; and by reason of his
ignorance, far too superstitious, to dare an attempt
to foist upon others fanciful and foundationless traditions. As science advances, and phenomena pass
from the domain of the unknown to that of the
known and understood, scepticism advances too, and
keeps pace with science ; while the beliefs of the
past are more and more treated with ridicule, or as
pretty fables only fit for poetical elaboration. Then
comes the time when imagination runs riot, loosed
from the shackles of responsibility ; and that which
once was a venerable record, degenerates into a

childish tale. Nevertheless, these myths, inherited by tradition from the days of ignorance, have always some kernel of truth imbedded in the quaint conglomerate, overlaid and, it may be, hidden away, and difficult to find, but still representing facts, and therefore not to be despised.

One of the most remarkable instances of truth being transmitted by tradition, through countless generations of ignorant repeaters, is afforded by the discoveries made in the present century by geologists. The earnest labours of geologists and comparative anatomists, have, step by step, demonstrated as an actual fact, the existence upon this earth, in prehistoric times, of certain monstrous beings which afterwards became extinct, but whose existence has been vouched by tradition handed down through thousands of years; but because these traditions have only been transmitted by the ignorant and superstitious, and there have been no facts wherewith to verify them, they came to be considered as wholly fabulous, and the mere creations of morbid imaginations.

It is now, however, proved beyond dispute that once upon a time there did exist on the earth beings such as these ignorant and superstitious people have talked about; huge monsters, who were not only tyrants of the ocean, but also of the shore.

Of these, the Ichthyosaurus had the vast proportions of the whale, enormous jaws, reaching six feet in length, and furnished with hundreds of shark-like teeth.[1] The Plesiosaurus "to the head of a lizard, united the teeth of the crocodile; a neck of enormous length, resembling the body of a serpent; a trunk and tail having the proportions of an ordinary quadruped, the ribs of a chameleon, and the paddles of a whale.[2] The Atlantosaurus, the largest land animal ever known to have existed, was of the same type, but was from fifty to sixty feet long, and standing thirty feet high.[3] Finally, the Pterodactyle, a monster resembling a bat or vampire, but having a head and jaws like the crocodile, filled with cruel teeth, eyes of enormous size, fitting it to fly by night, leather-like wings, from which projected fingers terminated by long hooks, forming a powerful paw, wherewith it could creep, or climb, or swim.[4] This monster was not a bat, nor a bird, but a veritable flying reptile, the incarnation of the legendary fiend who,

> O'er bog or steep, through strait, rough, dense or rare,
> With head, hands, wings, or feet, pursues his way,
> And swims, or sinks, or wades, or creeps, or flies.[5]

These monsters were not, like the huge though

---

[1] Buckland's "Geology," 166 *et seq.*   [2] *Ib.* 199.
[3] Wallace, "Island Life," 96.   [4] Buckland's "Geology," 219.
[5] "Paradise Lost," b. ii. 947.

THE ORIGINAL DRAGON

smaller animals of the present age,—the elephant, the hippopotamus, and the rhinoceros,—feeders on herbs, and without incentive to destroy life, except in self-defence : nor like whales, who feed on the smallest fish and molluscs they can find ; but truly ferocious, voracious, life destroying, and devouring reptiles— known to have attained gigantic dimensions, the flying reptiles nearly 30 feet from wing to wing, and the others 30, 40, 70 and 100 feet in length, and some of vast bulk, with jaws and teeth, so formed as to show them to have been in a high degree car-nivorous.[1] Naturalists are still able to recognize in the ocean races of animals—dwarfed and degenerate, it is true, but with sufficient distinctive charac-teristics to justify the conclusion—direct descendants of these monster reptiles. Add to this the fact recently discovered, that there *are* reptiles of the lizard or saurian order, which are venomous ;—estab-lishing as true, that which had long been regarded as an absurd superstition,—and another point may be scored to the traditional dragon.

Now what do we find in human tradition ? The Chaldeans tell us that Merodach fought with and conquered a monster, which came up from the deep covered with scales, furnished with wings, and armed with claws. In later times the legend passed into

---

[1] Buckland's " Geology," 229.

that of Bel and the Dragon, and from time to time reappears in such records as that of Michael the Archangel and Satan, and Saint George and the Dragon. The same legend appears in Greek mythology, in the combat between Zeus and Typhœus, although the horrors of the monster are magnified into a hundred heads and fiery eyes. Phœbus, who like Bel, was a sun-god, had a fight with Python, an enormous serpent, and the exploit is handed down in mythology. Horus, an Egyptian Bel, fights and overcomes Apophis, a monstrous reptile. Similar feats are recorded in almost every mythology that has assumed a definite form : Œdipus overcomes the devouring Sphinx, Bellerophon the Chimera : in Hindu mythology, the serpent Vritra is smitten, in that of Zoroaster there is Ahi, and in the modern Parsee, Zohak, both monsters of the same class : even Buddhism has its dragon fight, for when Kiouen-thsang returned to China, he brought with him a golden statue representing the Buddha conquering the Dragon.[1] The Scandinavians had echoes of the same traditions ; for there are combats with monsters of all sorts ; and in the sea which surrounds their world is the great Midgard serpent, who is to be slain at the end of the world by Thor. This great serpent still lives on in popular belief, as the great

---

[1] Max Müller, " Chips," i. 275.

sea-serpent, and has, even to this day, very respectable adherents.

In the book of Job we recognize in Leviathan, a creature more like the extinct saurians of the old world, than any crocodile recorded in historic times; and this Leviathan is treated as still existing in the days of David. In the 74th Psalm, Jehovah is spoken of as having broken the heads of the dragons in the waters, and the heads of Leviathan in pieces;[1] in Isaiah, as having wounded the dragon :[2] and pæans are sung on the anticipated punishment of "Leviathan, that crooked serpent," and the slaying of "the dragon that is in the sea :"[3] Finally, in the Apocalyptic vision, " I saw an angel come down from heaven, having the key of the bottomless pit and a great chain in his hand. And he laid hold on the dragon, that old serpent, which is the Devil, and Satan, and bound him."[4]

Do not these facts prove to demonstration that some individuals, at least, of the now extinct races of monsters, survived into times, when man not only existed, but was capable of passing on his experience to his descendants ? Combats with such monsters, and their destruction or flight, would be scenes of such terrific and enthralling interest, as not to be

---

[1] Ps. lxxiv. 13, 14. [2] Isaiah li. 9. [3] Isaiah xxvii. 1.
[4] Rev. xx. 1, 2,; and see Rev. xii. 7–9.

effaced from the memory of the beholders; and with such materials for tradition, the only wonder is that the popular conception of a dragon, framed on tradition, passed on through hundreds of generations should have not only retained its identity, but should be found to bear a most startling resemblance to the original, whose bones have slept for thousands of years in their stone encasement, and now come to light, as it were, almost for the purpose of proving the marvellous tenacity of tradition, and the honesty of those who passed it on.

All such traditions have had their origin in savage times, when man was too simple to indulge in conscious idealism. It is often argued that the monsters of tradition are personifications of the Deep, or of the Storm, or of the Desert wind, or of Rivers inundating their banks; and so no doubt they often are and have been: but the wholly uncultured human mind would be incapable of creating an ideal dragon; of building it up with limbs symbolical of their special contribution to the composite being, with composite ideal attributes. Such a process assumes an amount of intelligent reasoning and poetical idealism, which would not be combined in a savage nature. A savage might make an image of an animal, a snake, or a lion, the object of his worship; and he might embellish his image with a human head; and succeeding generations might improve upon the ideal,

until all sorts of monstrosities might be portrayed :
but it is not conceivable that such hap-hazard model-
ling would combine in one being so many of the characteristics of the pterodactyle as are found in the
dragon of tradition, unless the tradition itself had
been pregnant with the combination.

Mr. Conway writes : "The opinion has steadily
gained that the conventional dragon is the traditional form of some huge saurian. It has been
suggested that some of those extinct forms may have
been contemporaneous with the earliest men, and
that the traditions of conflicts with them, transmitted orally and pictorially, have resulted in preserving their forms in fable proximately."[1]

Man will idealize facts, and will also idealize
misinterpreted facts : he will then materialize his
ideals, and thus in time create a whole world of
imaginary facts; these imaginary facts settle down
and solidify, and in their turn become material for
idealization ; and so on *ad infinitum :* but whatever
may be built up afterwards, and however numerous
the stages of the edifice, the original starting-point
will not have been an ideal, but a fact. Man would
not personify the sea as a marine monster, unless he
believed in the existence of a marine monster in some
way associated with the sea : he would not idealize

---

[1] Conway, "Demonology," i. 320.

a river as a scaly reptile, with a weakness for sheep, unless he had seen or heard of a scaly reptile coming up out of a river and carrying off a sheep as prey. But when the idea of the river, and the devouring reptile once became associated, the transition was easy to an identification of the two ; and when the river burst its bounds, and swept away the flocks, it was natural enough to speak of the river as a dragon coming up out of its bed, and devouring the sheep as its prey.

Instances of composite beings occur abundantly in the mythologies of the world, and they are no doubt mostly attributable to the universal tendency to anthropomorphism, by which, in some cases, the forms of animals have been dignified by adding the attributes of man ; or in others, some special charac- teristics of man intended to be accentuated have been shown, by adding to the human form the attributes of certain animals. Of the former class are the serpents, bulls, horses and lions, with human heads : of the latter are the hawk-headed, ibis- headed and jackal-headed deities of Egypt ; the fish-tailed mermaidens and tritons, of marine habits and abode ; the pans and satyrs, with goat-like extremities and semi-bestial natures.

These animal-headed deities were at one time probably imagined in human form, attended by a hawk, an ibis, or a jackal ; as Jove was represented as attended by an eagle, and Odin by his ravens and dogs, and other deities by their own especial familiars : the mermaidens and tritons were closely associated in the mind with fishes, and the pans and satyrs with goats : and the composite ideals were the result. Professor Max Müller would perhaps call the earlier stage that of the monosyllabic ideal, and the composite form the agglutinative stage :[1] for his general principle would include this case :— " Everywhere amalgamation points back to combination, and combination back to juxtaposition."[2]

The Bible opens with the statement that, " In the beginning . . . . the earth was without form and void, and darkness was on the face of the deep." This represented the generally received opinion, that time was when our Earth did not exist, but Chaos reigned supreme ; when all the elements were mingled, formless, lifeless ; filling an abyss without bottom, extending in all directions without limits of any kind.

> The hoary deep ; a dark
> Illimitable ocean, without bound,
> Without dimension, where length, breadth and height,
> And time, and place are lost; where eldest Night
> And Chaos, ancestors of Nature, hold
> Eternal anarchy.[3]

---

[1] Max Müller, "Science of Religion," 154.
[2] Max Müller, "Chips," iv. 86.   [3] "Paradise Lost," b. 2.

This chaotic abyss was watery, but yet not exactly water, although often spoken of, for want of a better expression, as "the primordial waters." This idea finds expression in the Veda :—

> Nor Aught nor Nought existed; yon bright sky
> Was not, nor heaven's broad woof outstretched above.
> What covered all? what sheltered? what concealed?
> Was it the water's fathomless abyss?[1]

And in the Edda :—

> 'Twas Time's first dawn,
> When nought yet was,
> Nor sand nor sea,
> Nor cooling wave;
> Earth was not there,
> Nor heaven above.
> Nought save a void
> And yawning gulf,
> But verdure none.[2]

A germ of life is then believed to have come into existence, often spoken of as an egg—the mundane, or cosmic egg—which by degrees developed into the world fitted for the reception of living beings. The account of Creation in the first chapter of Genesis fairly represents the general idea of this development. First, a breath moved through the formless abyss, separating it into two elements, air and

---

[1] Max Müller, "Chips," ii. 195.
[2] Mallet, "Northern Antiquities," 401.

water; next, the advent of light caused another difference from universal darkness; the air developing still further, forced up the superincumbent water, until there was a firmament, an aërial space between waters above and waters below; the lower waters then recede from the centre, and the dry land appears. These waters produce creatures that have life, and flying fowl to people the air. The earth having brought forth vegetation now produces beasts of the earth, and creeping things, and man. The sun and moon and stars were made to serve the earth, and run their course within the hollow dome formed by the waters above the firmament. It was firmly believed, however, that Chaos continued to exist everywhere beyond the limits of this organized world, and it was assumed that any one sailing on the ocean, right away and far enough from the land, would reach the confines of the world, and enter on the realms of Chaos, where darkness, fog, and unsubstantiality reigned supreme.

At an early stage of the creation, and before Nature had finally settled down, it was believed that monsters of various forms had been created and fitted to live in the semi-obscurity of Chaos, only half dispelled: but that as the earth became more settled and light increased, these creatures, unable to bear this light, either perished or were driven into the misty circle of primeval Chaos. Berosus enumerates the monstrous forms which these beings assumed, and which in his time were portrayed in the Babylonian temples : men, with two or four wings, and with two faces, both male and female ; human figures with legs and horns of goats ; some with horses' feet, others with the hind quarters of a horse and the body of a man ; bulls with heads of men ; dogs with fourfold bodies, terminated with fishes' tails ; horses with heads of dogs ; men with heads of horses, and other animals with heads and bodies of horses, and tails of fishes. In short, creatures in which were combined the limbs of every species of animals. Besides these, were fishes, reptiles, serpents, and other monstrous animals which could assume each others' shape and countenance. All these were presided over by the goddess of Chaos, Tiamtu, the Thallath of Berosus.[1]

The Chaldean legends, recently exhumed, confirm these traditions and record the contest of Merodach —or Bel—the sun-god, with the monsters of Chaos, and their defeat. They either perished or were driven away into outer Chaos. The champion of Chaos was a dragon, a composite monster, with the tail, horns, claws, and wings of the medieval devil.[2]

In the gloomy land of the Cimmerians and the confines of Hades, these strange monsters were to be

---

[1] Smith's " Chaldean Genesis," Sayce, 35.   [2] *Ib.* 99, 113.

met; and not only there, but in any part of the universe which was conceived as beyond the pale of human habitation, the same weird creatures might be encountered. When Izdhubar undertook the journey to the land of the dead, in order to interview Hasisadra, the Chaldean Noah, scorpion-men were found guarding the gate of the sun; terrible in aspect, gigantic in stature, with their heads in heaven and their feet in Hades.[1]

Similar visions were encountered when Æneas approached the gates of Hades:—

> Of various forms, unnumbered spectres more;
> Centaurs and double shapes besiege the door:
> Before the passage horrid Hydra stands,
> And Briareus with all his hundred hands:
> Gorgons and Geryon with his triple frame,
> And vain Chimæra vomits empty flame.[2]

Hesiod records the birth of monstrous beings of various forms, Thaumas, Tiamat, the great deep: the winged harpies; Medusa and the Gorgons, serpent-headed; Echidna, half nymph, with dark eyes and fair cheeks and half serpent, huge, terrible and vast, speckled and flesh devouring; Cerberus, the flesh devouring fifty-headed dog of Hell; the Lernæan hydra, the hundred-headed monster, slaughtered by Hercules, a sun-god; Chimæra, a monster with three

---

[1] Smith's "Chaldean Genesis," by Sayce, 259.   [2] "Æneid," b. 6.

P

heads, one of a lion, another of a goat and the third of a serpent, slain by Bellerophon and Pegasus, the winged horse ; the Sphinx, a devouring, scaly dragon of the deep: the Nemæan lion, and a host of other monsters.[1]

The same idea is recognized in the semitic belief, that uncanny beings lurked in the outer deserts, where men did not penetrate at all, or did so only at great danger. The "place of dragons" is associated with the "shadow of death ;"[2] dragons are associated with the waters of the deep :[3] and are called upon with the deeps to praise Jehovah.[4] Isaiah wishing to describe the utter desolation and destruction which should come on Zion's enemies prophecies that—

> Their streams shall be turned into pitch,
> And the dust into brimstone,
> And the land thereof shall become burning pitch,
> It shall not be quenched night or day ;
> The smoke thereof shall go up for ever.

> Thorns shall come up in her palaces,
> Nettles and brambles in the fortresses thereof,
> And it shall be a habitation of dragons,
> And a court for ostriches.
> The wild beasts of the desert
> Shall also meet with the wild beasts of the island,
> And the satyr shall cry to his fellow.[5]

---

[1] "Hesiod," 265, &c.   [2] Ps. xliv. 19.   [3] Ps. lxxiv. 13.
[4] Ps. cxlviii. 7.   [5] Is. xxxiv.

Hesiod's monstrous beings are of various forms, and cannot be fairly associated with any ancestors of beings in actual life and known to man ; but the most terrible of all monsters, the oldest form and that which generated the greatest and most enduring dread, was the marine monster, with scales, and claws, and of enormous size and strength ; a relentless de-vourer, and with a cruel ruthless nature. The legends of such beings have always been numerous and per-sistent, and outnumber all other monster-legends put together. Their antiquity is clearly attested by their being mentioned in the oldest records that the world possesses,—they are the "great whales" of the history of creation in Genesis ; we have seen that the Chaldean creation tablets speak of them ; Hesiod tells us that the veil of Pandora was wrought with figures of sea-monsters, and, as everything connected with traditions of Prometheus, like the legend of Pandora, relates back to the earliest ages of which memories are embalmed in Greek mythology, this little record of female attire carries back mythical history into the remotest antiquity.

We have already referred to some of the oldest battles with these monsters, and pointed out the im-probability that such ideals should have been adopted, unless beings had at one time existed upon which the figure of speech could have been originally engrafted. These battles became in time the common property of all the epic poets of the world, and from them spread to the bards and troubadours, and even to the preachers of medieval times, furnishing subjects for heroic history, stirring romance and brilliant pageants.

St. Michael, the archangel (the lineal descendant of Merodach-Bel, the conquerer of the primeval monster of the deep), is represented as treading upon a dragon and piercing him with a spear.

St. George, the patron saint of England, although of doubtful identity, and unpleasantly associated with an Arian and not too scrupulous archbishop of Alexandria, is popularly accredited as a soldier champion of Christendom, who immortalized himself at Sylene, a city of Lydia, by his chivalrous and gallant exploits. Near Sylene was a stagnant lake or pond like a sea, wherein dwelt a dragon, who was so fierce and venomous that he terrified and poisoned the whole country. The people assembled to slay him, but when they saw him, his appearance was so horrible that they fled. Then the dragon pursued them even to the city itself, and the inhabitants were nearly destroyed by his very breath, and suffered so much, that they were obliged to give him two sheep every day to keep him from doing them harm. At length the number of sheep became so small, that they could only give him one sheep every day, and they were obliged to give him a man instead of the

other. Lots had eventually to be cast amongst all
the surviving inhabitants, and one day it fell upon
the king's daughter, and great was the lamentation
which ensued. When the fatal day for the sacrifice
of the king's daughter arrived, she, decked in bridal
dress, went out to meet the dragon. On the road
she fell in with St. George in full panoply and
mounted on his charger. After a brief explanation,
the dragon appeared on the scene, was encountered
and wounded by the Christian knight, bound by the
lady's girdle, and led like a "meke beest" into the
city. On condition of the king and 15,000 men becoming Christians, St. George slew the dragon ; his
remains were carted away, and a church dedicated to
our Lady and St. George was built to commemorate
the event.[1]

In Spenser's "Faërie Queene" we read of the
monster of Errour in its den :—

> Halfe like a serpent horribly displaide,
> But th' other halfe did woman's shape retaine,
> Most lothsom, filthie, foule, and full of vile disdaine.
> And as she lay upon the durtie ground,
> Her huge long taile her den all overspred,
> Yet was in knots and many boughtes upwound,
> Pointed with mortall sting.[2]

A furious fight takes place between this monster

[1] Hone's "Every-Day Book," April 23.
[2] Book 1, 14, 15.

and the hero-knight, ending in the defeat and death of the former.

A romance without some dragon or monster, was as rare as one without a valiant knight or a beautiful lady; but these characters were not confined to light literature, but reappear almost verbatim in the sublime imagery of Milton :—

> Before the gates there sat
> On either side a formidable shape;
> The one seem'd woman to the waist, and fair;
> But ended foul in many a scaly fold
> Voluminous and vast; a serpent arm'd
> With mortal sting.
> The other shape,
> If shape it might be call'd that shape had none
> Distinguishable in member, joint or limb;
> Or substance might be call'd that shadow seem'd,
> For each seem'd either; black it stood as night,
> Fierce as ten Furies, terrible as hell,
> And shook a dreadful dart; what seemed his head
> The likeness of a kingly crown had on.[1]

In Bunyan's " Pilgrim's Progress" we meet with a sort of dragon or monster in the person of Apollyon; hideous to behold, clothed with scales like a fish, wings like a dragon, feet like a bear, and a mouth like a lion.

A favourite subject for Chinese and Japanese painting and sculpture, is a dragon or monster very

---

[1] " Paradise Lost," b. 2.

much of the same type, and a monstrous representation of a dragon in the form of a huge saurian, still forms the central object at Japanese festivals.

All these are variants of the original monster type, changing and shifting in their characteristics, like the shadowy beings of which they are the representations : the sea-nymph is a very favourite form and constantly reappears ; but the dragon with scales and wings, claws and cruel teeth, is still more frequent, and has remained from age to age distinctly a ferocious, flying reptile, until the tradition has been justified by the discoveries of prosaic science.

The subject of monstrous beings necessitates a reference to the large and important class of the Pan and Satyr type.   A being in the form of a man above the waist, and of a goat or bull below, and with cloven hoofs and horns is found in the mythology of many nations ; and as this form has become consecrated to the medieval Devil, and still lives in the conception of the vulgar mind, a few moments of inquiry into the probable origin of the idea will not be out of place.

Like all other ideals of a kindred nature, that of the satyr was built up from a number of independent sources, and we should be mistaken if we expected to pitch upon a single root from which it could be shown to have sprung : it has, on the contrary, been the result of a long course of evolution. The final product of evolution may be, and often is, as different from the germ as the oak tree is from the acorn; and in the evolution of the satyr we probably have an example of this difference.

We have seen what a miserable and limited existence that of man was before he learned the use of artificial fire and light; when he had no better implements than roughly chipped flints; when he lived in holes and dens of the earth, and had to fight for sheer existence through the dark and dreary nights, unlighted and unwarmed, against the better equipped races of the brute creation: when his food was only fruit and uncooked roots and the raw flesh of such animals as he could overcome, and of the human enemies he could conquer. It is not to be supposed that these early undeveloped men were few in number, or limited in range: on the contrary, careful search and intelligent deduction have shown beyond dispute, that these early races of men were probably spread over the whole world, and that they were so numerous as to leave recognizable traces of their existence in almost every country; traces in the form of flints, undoubtedly shaped by the hand of man, and although buried for countless ages in beds of river drift now far below the present surface, yet sown broadcast, and in such profusion, as to be constantly found when searched for by the very few

who are competent to recognize their character.
Europe has been of course the principal field of
research, and has not unnaturally been most fruitful in results : but these paleolithic implements have
also been found in Palestine, Assyria, India and
Japan ; in Algeria, Egypt, and other parts of
Africa ; throughout the whole of America ; in
Australia and Polynesia :[1] every year reports of
similar discoveries in fresh countries are made to the
scientific world. The Danish Museum alone contains
30,000 stone implements, and the number is constantly increasing.[2]

If we start with the whole world teeming with
men of this primitive type; and then realize the first
spark of a civilization appearing at some one point,
where the power of a higher culture took root and
then radiated, we can understand how this power
of civilization as it radiated drove back the savage
races. It is the instinct and the universal custom
of the more powerful to drive the less powerful away
from the most favoured districts of the earth, and to
leave their inferiors to shift as best they can in
those parts where Nature is less kind, and life more
hard to sustain : and so it came about, that as stage

---

[1] "Prehistoric Times," by Sir J. Lubbock, 103 ; and see Prof.
Boyd Dawkins' "Address to the Section of Anthropology at
Southampton," 1882, British Association.

[2] "Prehistoric Times," 75.

after stage of civilization was attained, and as wave after wave of culture swept over the world, the primitive savage who had before roamed unopposed through the earth—only meeting everywhere with the same dead level of ignorance—was driven further and further from the centres of enlightenment. When history first came into existence, the rudest savage was only to be found in those inhospitable confines of the then known world, which were deemed the border-land of chaos: the northern lands of mist and darkness: the rock-girt or distant island: the burning sandy desert with its lurid horrors: the impenetrable forests, backed by perpetual mountain snows: jungles or fastnesses, where the tangled labyrinth of vegetation, the tiger and the serpent, the deadly miasma and the treacherous swamp, combined to create inaccessibility. This process had been repeated, as each fresh development had been established, and it is certain that many succeeding strata of savages have been completely crowded out of the world and become extinct, by the ever widening circle of civilization :—each crowded out by a succeeding race, more civilized, and therefore more powerful, although only so by comparison ; and itself doomed to be crowded out by another race, relatively superior. This is the natural history of so-called aborigines ; but recorded history only cuts in at a period when the aborigines for the time being represented a survival of untold ages, and however low the survivors might be found, there had certainly in the past been vast depths of human existence infinitely lower still, the representatives of which had been swept away, and which can only now be realized by analogical deduction.

Analogy however furnishes us with no uncertain data from which to deduce the course of past events on this subject. The natives of Australia, the Bushmen of South Africa, the Veddas of the interior of Ceylon, the Nagas and other hill tribes of the Indian Peninsula, and the Andamanese islanders, all probably represent remnants of populations which once were general, but which have been driven into their present narrow limits; and which, in spite of the efforts of the Aborigines Protection Society, are doomed to early extinction. How many of such races have died out in recent times! unable, like the pre-adamite creatures of Chaldean mythology, to endure the light:—in this case, the light and power of civilization.

These tribes are so shy, and so jealous of observation, that we hardly have time to acquaint ourselves with their character and habits, before we see them melt away and disappear, as it were, under our very eyes. We find them physically and socially, and at times even mentally, so different from the races which now hold possession of the world, as to make them seem to belong to a different nature, and to lead us sometimes to doubt their human attributes; but if we could transport our standpoint of observation to the dawn of tradition, that is to say, to a period when the most cultured race then existing, had not long, if at all, emerged from the state in which the Australians and the Veddas now are, we could well imagine the human beings, then living on the fringe of habitable space, and compelled so to live in consequence of their marked inferiority to the dominant races, then of the Australian and Vedda type, to be many degrees nearer the brute, and immeasurably more removed from the average human type than those Australians and Veddas now are. We have seen, too, how persistent tradition can be, and there is nothing fanciful in supposing that the traditions of monsters of semi-human form, said to have inhabited the border-land of chaos, were founded upon the existence of beings of monstrous and uncouth shapes, which had been seen lurking about the far distant and inhospitable confines of the known world, or hiding away in fastnesses and inaccessible places. That these beings should be invested with exaggerated deformities, is not at all surprising, considering the difficulties of observation, and the well founded sense of danger in a close encounter, for it is to be supposed that these semi-brutal men, would have habits more savage and brutal than their less savage neighbours, and instincts which would make them naturally turn their hand against their enemies and oppressors.

It has not been at all an uncommon tradition respecting low races of men, that they were descended from apes, and that they had and sometimes still have tails : but this seems to arise from an idea of the general fitness of things, and as an indication of the low esteem in which the inferior race is held by their more cultured neighbours. This subject has been carefully examined by Mr. Tylor in his "Primitive Culture," and he points out that there are even now, races who are ready to admit their own descent from apes.[1] That man and apes are descended from some common ancestral form, which existed at a very remote period, is now generally admitted by evolutionists ; but it is as incorrect to say that man is descended from an ape, as it would be to maintain that the English are descended from the Hindus, because they happen to claim a common ancestry in the original Aryan stock, or that a man is descended from his second cousin because they both happen to have had the same great-grandfather.

The origin of the myth of the Satyr, is however more enveloped in mystery, and cannot be explained

---

[1] Vol. i. 378 *et seq.*

by a supposed reference to savage and uncouth tribes, although these latter may have in a great degree contributed to the accumulation of confused notions on the subject.

Probably the oldest record of a satyr is that of Hea-bani, the companion and friend of Izdhubar, the solar hero of the Chaldean legends. Hea-bani is represented with an upright human form, but with the feet, tail and horns of a bull: he is said to have lived in a cave among the wild animals of the forest, and was supposed to possess wonderful knowledge both of Nature and of human affairs. He is a composite being, half man, half bull. Now for some reasons, not understood, but undoubtedly existant, the bull was, in the Chaldean mythology, adopted as an embodiment of divine power; indeed one of Hea-bani's greatest feats was slaying "the bull of heaven," which Anu, the god of heaven, had created at the request of Istar, and whereby she hoped to avenge herself on Izdhubar, for his indifference to her. The bull with human face occurs again and again in Ninevitish and Babylonian monuments, and such figures represented powerful protecting genii.[1] The name "Hea-bani" means "created by Hea:" Hea was the god of the

---

[1] Examples of these are to be seen at the Assyrian Court at the Crystal Palace.

abyss,[1] and of wisdom—of deep things—the only deity who could unloose the fetters forged by spells and incantations. Hea-bani, then, the created of the god of wisdom, the super-magical deity, was therefore a semi-god; superhuman help was wanted by Izdhubar, and only such help was to be found with a superhuman being, like Hea-bani, who combined divine and human knowledge, and who was therefore conceived as having a composite body blended of the two natures. In passing, it may be noted, that not only was the bull adopted as a form for god-like creatures, but the cow was still more widely identified with the moon-goddess in the mythologies of many nations: the moon's crescent has been thought to suggest horns and account for the myth, but it is probable that the true origin lies further out of view than that.

The Hebrews believed in the existence of satyrs

---

[1] The abyss answers to the "water under the earth" in the second commandment of the Decalogue. The Hebrews were prohibited from making the likeness of any creature in the abyss, which according to Berosus were so plentifully portrayed on the walls of the Babylonian temples. The same "imagery" caused Ezekiel so much disturbance when he saw it transferred to the Temple of Jerusalem—"every form of creeping things, and abominable beasts" (Ez. viii. 10); these were the inhabitants of the "great and wide sea, wherein are things creeping innumerable, both small and great beasts" (Ps. civ. 25); the whales and living creatures which move (creep) and which the waters had brought forth on the fifth day of creation (Gen. i. 21).

in the remote deserts—their idea of the borders of chaos—but they had progressed one step nearer the later ideal, by making their satyr a compound of man and goat. The distinctive features of their satyr however was, that he was "a hairy one;" and we accordingly find the same term applied to Esau, the hairy man,[1] as was applied to some of the deities worshipped by Jeroboam, who "ordained him priest for the high places, and for the *devils*" (hairy ones), "and for the calves which he had made."[2] And Isaiah speaking of utter desolation in a passage already quoted, emphasises his prophecy by describing a place as the abode of satyrs, or hairy ones.[3] It is interesting to note, that Esau, called one of the "sè-irim," or hairy demons, was *red*, and therefore surnamed Edom (*red*), that he sold his birthright for a mess of *red* pottage, and that he was specially assigned Mount *Seir* as a home for his descendants : we have seen that *red* was a special colour for evil spirits.

It has been suggested that the horns popularly attributed to the Devil may have originated with the aureole of a divine being, still lingering round his head after his fall from heaven, and that the brightness of Moses' face, when he came down

---

[1] Gen. xxvii. 11.   [2] 2 Chron. xi. 15.   Moloch had a calf's head.
[3] Is. xxxiv. 14; and see xiii. 21.

from Mount Sinai was of the same nature, and that this also has been called horns: both Satan and Moses being both represented as horned, and both from a similar cause.[1]   But this explanation of the Devil's horns would have seemed far-fetched, even had we not been able to show by records, probably older than Moses, and certainly older than the Pentateuch, that beings closely akin to the Devil were already being depicted with horns, hoofs, and a tail.   These same beings, with but slight modifications, were always kept alive in mythology as Pans, Priaps, Satyrs and Fauns, and when a bodily shape was wanted for the arch-enemy of mankind, this seemed the most appropriate and was adopted accordingly.

The addition of dragon's wings to the satyr form was a further development, arising from the concurrent claims of the two ideals, and again "juxtaposition led to combination."

---

[1] Conway's "Demonology," vol. i. 19.

Q

IX.

CONCLUSION.

At the outset, the Devil was defined as the Supreme Spirit of Evil, and Evil was identified with Opposition. In accordance with that view, we found that the Satan of the Hebrews was an "adversary," a spy and informer, an accuser of man to his God, and, as such, man's opponent. We saw how Chaldean and Persian influences gradually modified the ideal, and created the Satan of the New Testament, in whom were combined attributes which made him more and more hateful and formidable, until he became a shroud of sombre darkness, overshadowing and oppressing the whole moral world : he became more and more the enemy—the opponent of man.

We have traced the lineage of spiritual beings of most varied characters, with whom the Earth and the Abyss, Heaven and Hell, have been peopled, and whose histories have gradually melted into that of the Christian Devil ; and we have shown that in many instances these beings were quondam gods of high renown. We have examined the history of Hell and its monarchs, all now deposed by Satan, who has usurped the sole control of the nether world. We have found him clothed with fire, physical and moral, and a form derived from the most remote antiquity, when monsters, at first the denizens, and afterwards the types of a half-chaotic world, were strong in opposition to mankind, and waged a not unfairly balanced warfare for supremacy. We have seen how all these lines have from time to time converged to build up the great embodiment of the modern Satan, and to perfect him in the possession of every known or imagined evil, physical or moral, which the universe of Nature and of thought could formulate. The result has been a Protean being, shifting and changing with the point of view, and never seen by any two alike. Each one who thinks of a Devil at all, fancies him at his own will, and has such a vast variety of materials from which to draw, that he can construct with ease an ideal quite special to himself. No dogmatic definition of the Devil would meet with general adoption, or if adopted in one age would pass muster in the next; and it is a fact that the ideal has shifted with the age, and still shifts and changes with every breath of doctrine, religious or philosophical.

The Hebrews had their Satan, and the Jews a revised ideal. Asmodeus came from Persia, was

adopted by the Rabbins, and the mantle of Ahriman
fell upon him : the product was the Satan of the
New Testament. The cultured systems of Egypt,
Greece and Rome, and the venerable myths of
Babylon, all contributed their quota, before the
arch-enemy of the Christian faith assumed his final
shape :—in the Apocalypse the Devil is truly poly-
morphous.

Even in the Christian Church the form was still
always changing, and was not tied down to fixed
tradition. The medieval monks did not realize a
Hebrew Satan, who passed half his time in heaven ;
nor a Rabbinical Asmodeus, who could be mistaken
for King Solomon ; but they made their Devil black
like the sooty Vulcan, and gave him horns and hoofs
like the Satyrs and Pans, with breath of fire and
brimstone, like the Chimera and Typhœus of their
classic lore. The Apollyon of Bunyan's " Pilgrim's
Progress " is not the monkish Devil, nor the king of
locusts of the Bible, but a foul fiend, conscientiously
built up with biblical materials found in the visions
of Daniel and the Apocalypse. Few amongst us now
would think of the Devil in either of these forms, or
in any bodily form at all, and would only accord him
personality as the great spirit of evil. The latest
guide to popular knowledge broadly lays it down
that " the idea of the Devil certainly no longer hulks
in Christian thought as it once did, nor is his reign

the recognized influence that it once was over human life and experience."[1]

In truth, Satan has gradually lost his mythology, his legions of demons have dropped away, and he himself is melting into an abstraction and dying out of view—an abstraction, like Milton's description of Death, "a shape that shape has none," which is almost too ideal to keep a personality, and seems gradually, but certainly, relaxing its hold upon popular belief.

The existence of such a being as Satan, without a dualism of good and evil, such as the Persian creed maintained, is admitted to be a mystery, by all who hold the doctrine : the existence of evil itself, under the control of an omnipotent and benevolent God, is part of the same great mystery. Whether such a mystery admits of a solution, and whatever such solution may be, it is quite clear that many of the attributes of the orthodox Devil are inherited from the ancestors whose natures we have been discussing.

The ploughman, who, in his nightmare, dreams of the Devil, would no doubt still see a black, uncouth human form furnished with horns and hoofs and tail—he would see an exaggerated satyr. Or he would encounter a scaly dragon belching forth flames

---

[1] " Encyc. Brit." title " Devil."

from his jaws, gaping and bristling with hideous fangs, flapping his monstrous bat-like wings, and clawing and clutching at his prey—the monsters and dragons of primeval times would be the parents of his vision. The man smitten with palsy or with fever, bowed down with repeated strokes, and sinking in despair : the father grieving over the mental alienation of his child, or the blighting of his fields ; the wife who sees her husband distraught with drink ; the seaman who, caught in a cyclone, sees the " Flying Dutchman" cross his bows, riding on the storm ; the terror-stricken Sepoys in Afghanistan recounting how their Ghazi enemies ride horses who vomit fire and brimstone : All these confess the agency of demons, possessing or tormenting the body, or the mind, or the elements, or the enemy ; just as the old Turanians would have done in their day, and the Negro, Tartar or Red Indian still would do.

Many a gambler, debauchee or bravo, maddened with excitement, reckless as to consequences, yet steeped in superstition, whose very object and pursuit forbid appeal to any god or saint, will invoke the Devil, and claim his aid ; with much the same notion as suggested that Solomon of old sought out Asmodeus to help him build the Temple, and which drove Saul, Æneas and others, to seek the aid of witches, sorceresses and sibyls. The Trolls and Kobolds of our ancient homes oscillated between mischief and good nature : they would help their friends, and petulantly punish slights or inattention to their wants. Our word "devilry" smacks of Loki, Mercury and Puck, and, light as the word may be in application, its root is plain enough.

The devils and demons have now their home in Hell, where their office is to torment the souls of the wicked dead ; and Satan is their undisputed prince. But these devils and demons are only the successors of the spirits of the ancient Hades and Tartaros, who were under the sway of Pluto and Proserpine, and are indeed the Jinns and Genii of Arabian Tales. Satan is but Pluto in disguise, the King of Hell and ruler of the fire of Tartaros. He is also the master of the world's great subterranean smithy, and like Loki, Vulcan, Hephaestos, Asmodeus, and "le Diable Boiteux" of Le Sage, limps through existence as all other ideal devils are made to do.

The Bible tells us little or nothing as to the organization of Hades (Hell), or of Gehenna (Tartaros), but the orthodox interpretation of the little that is told, regards neither place as the permanent abode of any good thing : it is essentially a place prepared for the Devil and his angels. The Hades of the Assyrians, Egyptians and the Classics is much more minutely described, and we always find it presided over by a veritable god, and not an evil spirit—a god, stern and relentless, but still not evil ; and through the traditions of centuries, and the gloom of the Bible's imperfect light, we can still recognize in Satan the same character as the judges Osiris and Rhadamanthus, Dionysos and Pluto, a dark survival, bereft of their judicial virtues, now only the divine minister of justice, execrated and himself condemned, but still receiving and consigning to everlasting flames the souls which he has won.

The modern Christian, however, pays but little heed to the minor fiends and devils, and only realizes the one Devil, Satan, the arch-fiend ; ever present at the right hand and the left, reading the inmost thoughts, perceiving the first symptom of declension, with aptest skill inserting the thin end of the wedge into the slightest chink of the spiritual or moral armour, and, given the slightest leverage, able to apply power overwhelming and irresistible ; power which nothing human can withstand, and requiring the conjunction of the human will to invoke, and God Himself to exert a super-human strength to countervail : in fine, a being omnipresent, omniscient, and so near omnipotency as only to be overpowered by God Himself.   Do we not trace in this being, the Archangel, the deity, the once almost co-equal god ; the Ahriman of Persian dualism, warring against God, conquering and being conquered in turns ? Does not the Christian,—groaning in spirit at his own depravity, finding a law in his members warring against the law of his mind, wrestling and succumbing, fighting and conquering,—recognize in fact while he denies in form, that the Ahriman of the Persian dualism is the foundation of the Satan, in whom he believes, and, by his very terror, proclaim him only second to his God ?

PEDIGREE OF THE DEVIL.*

THE HEAVENS.

Deuce—a little devil—a common English expression for the Devil.
└**Deus**—a god or genius (Latin).
   └**Zeus**—the god or great spirit of the Heavens—or the firmament itself (Greek).
     └**Deva**—a spirit or shining one (Sanskrit).
       └**Dyaus**—the heavens—the bright expanse of the firmament (Sanskrit).

> NOTE.—The above are names belonging to the Aryan group of languages; the following names of gods and spirits also occur in the same group, and are of common origin :--
>
> **Dyaus pitār** (Sanskrit), **Zeus pater** (Greek), **Jupiter** (Latin)—*Heaven father.*
>
> **Theos** (Gr.), **Deus** (Lat.), **Diewar** (Lithuanian), —*God.*
>
> **Zio** (Old German), **Tyr** (Old Norse), **Tiw** (Anglo-Saxon)—*God.*
>
> **Dies** (Lat.), **Dyu** (Sansk.), **Day** (English)— *Daylight or Heaven-light.*
>
> **Zen** (Gr.), **Zenos** (Gr.), **Janus** (Lat.), **Dianus** (Lat.), **Diana** (Lat.), **Divine** (English).
>
> **Devel** (Gypsy)—*God.*
>
> **Dev** (old Persian)—*Demon.*
>
> **Deev** (mod. Persian)—*Fiend.*
>
> **Devil** (English).

---

* This is a key to the Genealogical figure in the Frontispiece.

GOD.

Bogle—a frightful spectre of evil influence (English and Scotch).
— Bug—a spectre such as that of death (Shakespeare).
— Bôg—a god (Slavonic).
— Bhaga—lord of fate (Hindu).
— Baga—the supreme being (Assyrian).

SPIRITS.

Puck—the typical house-spirit—a mischievous spirit, generally
described as an uncouth dwarfish figure (Shakespeare).
— Pouke—an evil spirit (Spenser).
— Pug—a fiend (Ben Jonson).
— Puk—a goblin (Friesland).
— Puki—an evil spirit (Iceland).
— Pixy—a mischievous, misleading fairy (Devonshire).
— Pooka—an evil spirit (Irish).
— Pwcca—an evil spirit (Welsh).
—— Elves (Alfs) — little semi-spiritual beings, of beautiful
form, much given to singing and dancing, and ex-
ercising magical powers (Scandinavian).
— House-spirits—dwarfish spirits, who busy themselves
in petty household matters for small pittances
of food, and bringing luck if well treated, but
seldom visible.
— Familiar spirits—evil spirits, bound to attend and
obey when called up.
— Penates—household gods of the ancient Romans.
— Heroes—spirits of deceased men, deified
and endued wth extraordinary powers
(Greek).
— Giants—mythological beings of great and
supernatural powers and dimensions.
— Trolls—small beings of uncouth human form, gifted
with magic powers, living in mounds or rocks,
much given to dancing, and skilled metal-
workers (Scandinavian).
— River-drift men—earliest known race of men—of

small stature—living in caves and underground dwellings— and traditionally credited with magical powers.

└─**Aborigines** —the first men who, appeared on the earth.

├─ **Dwarfs**—the trolls of English folk-lore.

└─ **Hill-people**—a class of spirits who, having rebelled against heaven, were condemned to live inside hills.

├─ **Duergar**—dwarfs produced from, and living under and in the earth, skilled in metal-working (Gothic).

├─ **Titans**—an early race of powerful gods, but overpowered by their successors, and condemned to imprisonment under the earth.

├─ **Rephaim**—the Titans of the Hebrews— antediluvian "great ones" cast into Sheol, under the earth and there imprisoned.

├─ **Fallen angels**—angels that sinned, cast down to hell, and reserved in chains under darkness, for judgment (New Testament).

├─ **Maskim**—the seven subterranean spirits of the Chaldeans, who once rebelled against heaven, dreaded for their great power.

└─ **Earth Spirits**—aboriginal gods, superseded by the gods of heaven, but still dreaded and feared for their magical powers.

├─ **Fairies**—inhabitants of Faërie, the realm of enchantment, latterly applied to the Fays and Elves, after they combined to form only one people— especially associated in folk-lore with the destiny of children.

- **Fays**—semi-spiritual beings described in the romances of the middle ages, as exercising enchantments, creating illusions—and especially influencing the fate of children.
- **Fates**—three female deities who determine human destiny at the time of birth.
- **Sibyls**—women gifted with the knowledge of destiny and oracular prophecy.
- **Nornir**—the fates of Scandinavian mythology, and with similar powers and practices.
- **Hathors**—Egyptian deities who attended the birth of children and foretold their destinies.
  - **Fate**—the settled course of future events, which even the gods themselves cannot change.
- **Furies**—avenging deities, with grim attributes, and associated with serpents.
- **Erinys**—the Greek furies.
- **Gorgons**—deities of magical powers, with serpents instead of hair: beholders of the face being turned into stone.
  - **Spells**—methods of binding by occult power through the employment of a form of words, or other ceremony overriding ordinary divine power.
- **Siduri** and **Sabitu**—Sorceresses who encountered Izdhubar on his travels, barring his way to the waters of the great deep.
  - **Magic**—supernatural influence exercised by inferior divinities or mortals by means of occult knowledge.
- **Asuras**—the good spirits of the Hindu religion, the bad spirits of the Persian religion.
- **Devas**—the good spirits of the Persian religion the bad spirits of the Hindu religion.

 — **Jinns**—spirits of smokeless fire, created before man, rebellious and punished (Arabian).

 — **Sheytâns**—devils — the offspring of Iblis, a specially rebellious Jinn (Arabian).

 — **Deevs**—Persian Jinns—wielding powers of enchantment, and malignant.

 — **Genii**—attendant spirits associated with individuals and influencing them for good or evil.

 — **Peris**—Persian female Jinns of enchanting beauty and supernatural powers.

 — **Dryads**—nymphs of woods and trees—fond of dancing and merry making.

 — **Sirens**—sea-nymphs, half women, half fish, decoying to destruction by their melodious voice.

 — **Naiads**—nymphs of the water, presiding over rivers, brooks and springs.

 — **Nymphs**—beings of a semi-spiritual and semi-human nature, gifted with magical powers, and remarkable for their hair.

 — **Mermaids**—mythical beings of the middle ages, half women, half fish, with flowing hair, and sweet voices.

 — **Lorelei**—German mermaids.

CHAOS AND THE ABYSS OF PRIMORDIAL WATERS.

Leviathan—a monster of the deep—a typical opponent of, and slain by, Jehovah, the consuming fire (Hebrew).

 — **Midgard serpent**—the great serpent inhabiting the ocean, which encircles the earth—to be slain by Thor, the god of fire, at the end of the world (Scandinavian).

 — **Sea serpent**—a great serpent supposed by some to inhabit the ocean, even in modern days.

 — **Vritra**—a devouring monster,—slain by Indra, the god of lightning (Vedic).

— **Apophis**—the great serpent of evil, inhabiting the infernal Nile,—to be slain by Horus (Ancient Egyptian).

— **Typhœus**—monster conquered by Zeus, the god of the thunderbolt (Greek).

— **Python**—a mythical monster, slain by Apollo (Greek).

— **Sphinx**—monster destroyed by Œdipus (Greek).

— **Hydra**—monster destroyed by Hercules (Greek).

— **Chimera**—a composite monster, destroyed by Bellerophon (Greek).

— **Echidna**—a monster slain by Argos (Greek).

— **Ahi**—the throttling serpent (Vedic).

— **Tiamtu**—the dragon conquered by Bel-Merodach, who wielded the thunderbolt (Babylonian).

— **The Deep**—Primordial chaos, personified in Tiamtu, Tiamat, Thaumas, Thallath, and all mythical dragons and sea-monsters.

— **Monsters**—composite beings—bred of the mighty deep and outer darkness—inimical to ordered existence.

— **Abzu**—the Chaldean primordial deep—the bottomless pit.

— **The Abyss**—the universal pre-organic condition of all space—and the condition of all space beyond the explored boundaries of the world.

— **Saurians**—such as the Ichthyosaurus, Plesiosaurus, Atlantosaurus, inhabitants of the world at the time it emerged from a state of chaos into light and order.

DEATH.

Hela—the goddess of death (Scandinavian).

— **Halja**—the black one (Gothic).

— **Kali**—the wife of Siva, the god of destruction (Hindu).

— **Death**—darkness, coldness and destruction.

FIRE.

— **Jove**—the god of the thunderbolts (Latin).

— **Zeus**—the same (Greek).

— **Thor**—the god of the thunderbolts (Scandinavian).

— **Indra**—the same (Hindu).

—— **Seraph**—a fiery serpent flashing from heaven, and guarding the throne of Jehovah (Hebrew).

— **The Fire of Heaven**—*Lightning.*

Mephistopheles—the personification of cultured vice (Goethe).

— **Asmodeus** — the demon of fiery lust—the prince of the demons (Rabbinic).

— **Aschmedai**—the lustful demon of Tobit.

— **Aëshma-daëva**—the spirit of impure fire (Zend).

— **Impure Fire**—the fire of moral depravity.

— **Sheytâns**—Arabian devils—offspring of Iblis (darkness), a rebel Jinn.

— **Jinns**—spirits of fire—offsprings of Samaël (**Death**) and Lilith.

— **Lilith**—the first wife of Adam (Rabbinic).

Lust—the characteristic of primeval religion.

— **Goblins**—the English form of the German Kobolds.

— **Kobolds**—German dwarf spirits of fiery attributes.

— **Loki**—the god of subterranean fire (Scandinavian).

— **Hephaestos**—the same (Greek).

— **Vulcan**—the same—the great metal-worker (Latin).

— **Tubal-cain**—the first instructor of metal-working (Hebrew).

—— **Internal Fire**—mining, smelting and metal-working.

MONARCHS AND JUDGES OF HELL.

Pluto—god of the underworld, and of everything subterranean.

— **Hades**—god of the invisible world, and of the dead.

— **'Aïdes**—invisible, unseen (Greek word).

— **Invisible**—state of the souls of the dead as contrasted with the visibility of the body in life.

— **Bit-hadi**—the Assyrian for " house of eternity."

— **House of Eternity**—the grave.

Rhadamanthus—one of the judges, and a tormentor of the dead.

— **Rho-t-amenti**—Osiris (Rā), the sun, as judge, in Hades (Amenti) (ancient Egyptian).

— **Dionysus**—the sun, as worshipped by the Arabians.

└─ **Dian-nisi**—the judge of men—the sun in Hades—with his searching light (Assyrian).

— **Yama**—god of hell and justice (Hindu).

— **Yami**—spirit of darkness (Vedic).

— **Yima**—king of Paradise (Iranian).

— **O Yama**—chief of the demons (Japan).

└─ **Amma**—God of Hell (Sintoo, Japan).

DARKNESS.

Ahriman—the spirit of evil, light being the ideal of good (ancient Persian).

└─ **Anra-mainyu**—the evil principle, the creator of Darkness (Zend).

└─ **Darkness**—evil as opposed to light as good.

DEMIGODS.

Medieval devil—grotesque ideal of the Devil, with goat-like horns, legs and hoofs, and a tail.

— **Priaps**—rural deities, with sensual and obscene attributes.

— **Pans**—rural deities, with goat-like horns, hoofs and legs, and a tail, much given to music (Greek).

— **Fauns**—sylvan or rural deities, human in form, but with goat's tail, horns and pointed ears, addicted to dancing and music (Roman).

└─ **Satyrs**—sylvan deities in form like Pans, distinguished for lasciviousness and riot.

└─ **Hea-bani**—Chaldean mythical being, half man, half bull (bull being the ideal of deity), with horns, tail, legs and hoofs of bull—living apart from mankind, and gifted with magical powers.

└─ **Demigods**—beings partaking of the nature of the gods and man.

THE SUN.

Beelzebub—the prince of the devils (New Testament).

└ Beel-zebul—the dung-god, a title of derision (Hebrew).

   └ Baal-zebub—the god of Ekron—the lord of flies (Old Testament).

      └ Baal—the supreme god of Canaanites and Phœnicians.

        ├ Bel—the great national deity of the Babylonians—the creator—afterwards identified with the sun.

        ├ Apollo—the sun worshipped as a deity.

        ├ Phœbus—the same.

        ├ Helios—the same.

        └── The Sun—the source of light and heat, and the vivifier of Nature.

Taous—figure of a mythical peacock worshipped by the Yzedis—the devil worshippers of Mesopotamia.

├ Taus—the Sabæan Tammuz.

   ├ Tammuz—the sun at night passing through the underworld (Syrian).

     └ Damuzi—the same (Assyrian).

      └ Duzi—The same (Chaldean).

       └ The Sun (in Hades).

├ Adonis—the sun alternating between the upper world and Hades.

├ Dianysos—the god of fertility—of joy and sadness alternating with the seasons.

├ Rokh—mythical bird in Arabian tales—evidently related to Taous.

├ Phœnix—mythical bird which periodically dies and revives again.

Herne the Hunter—an English legendary fiend.

└ Wild huntsman—a German fiend who hunts with a pack of hell-hounds.

244 THE PEDIGREE OF THE DEVIL.

- **Odin**—the hunter of the boar in the Scandinavian Valhalla
  —formerly the god of the sky.
- **Nimrod**—the mighty hunter before the Lord (Genesis).
- **Heroulos** the mighty performer of a zodiacal cycle of
  works (Greek).
- **Izdhubar**—the mighty hunter and performer of a zodiacal
  cycle of works (Chaldean).
  - **Mass of Fire**—the meaning of "Izdhubar"—really
    the sun—which travels through a zodiacal cycle
    in the heavens.

DESTRUCTION.

- **Abaddon**—destruction—the angel of the bottomless pit, the
  abyss (Revelations).
  - **Locusts**—typical of destruction—Abaddon being their prince.
    - **Destruction** very completely accomplished by locusts.
- **Apollyon**—the Greek form of Abaddon—a monster with scales
  like a fish, wings like a dragon, feet like a bear, and the
  mouth of a lion (Bunyan's "Pilgrim's Progress").
  - **Dragon**—a mythical reptilian monster, with wings, scales,
    claws, and horrid mien and jaws.
    - **Pterodactyle**—a primeval winged reptile, of enormous
      size, fitted for flying, creeping and swimming,
      powerful, cruel and voracious.

ANCESTORS.

- **Lares**—spirits of deceased persons who watch over the living
  (Roman).
- **Manes**—spirits of deceased ancestors inhabiting Hades, occasion-
  ally brought up again by sorcery.
- **Ghosts**—apparitions of deceased persons.
- **Vampyres**—souls of the dead, who at night feed on the blood of
  the living (Eastern Europe).
  - **Bats**—some kinds are said to suck the blood of sleeping men.
- **Brownies**—family spirits receiving sacrifices (Orkneys).

WATER.

Old Nick—a common English name for the Devil.
└ **Nikke**—a Norse and Dutch sea-demon—"The Flying Dutchman."
- **Nixy**—a diminutive water-demon.
- **Kelpie**—a water-horse carrying away and devouring the unwary (Scotland).
- **Merman**—a spirit living under the sea.
- **Riverman**—an elf, frequenting rivers.

Scratch—a common name for the Devil.
└ **Skratti**—"the roarer," an Icelandic storm demon.

SUN-RAYS—GOD'S MESSENGERS.

Lucifer—"light-bearing"—the day-star, which fell from heaven (Isaiah)—a typical devil (Milton).
- **Merodach**—servant or messenger of the gods—guide of the dead in Hades—a mediator—conqueror of the dragon (Babylonian).
  - **Marduk**—the same.
    └── **Silik-muludug**—the Accadian Marduk.
- **Mercury**—messenger of the gods—conductor of souls in the infernal regions — patron of dishonesty and trickery (Latin).
- **Hermes**—the Greek Mercury.
- **St. Michael**—an archangel (chief messenger) of Jehovah—the conqueror of Satan (Revelations)—a mediator (Origen).
  ──────────── **Messenger of the Gods**—the rays of the sun descending from heaven to earth and penetrating into the darkness of Hades and there constituting a guide.

CALAMITIES.

Storms—personified as Rudra, "the roarer" (Vedic), **Vayu, the** wind-god (Vedic), **Vul** and **Rimmon**, the air-god (Assyrian).

Loka-phayu, angels of tempests (Buddhist). Maruts, storm-gods (Vedic), &c.

Drought—personified as Typhon, the fiery wind (Greek), Azazel, the desert (Moslem), the scape-goat (Hebrew), &c.

Pestilence—personified as Namtar, the plague-demon (Chaldean), and many other forms of disease-demons—and also destroy-ing angels.

Famine—all natural obstacles to the procuring of food.

PRIMEVAL GODS.

Kronos—the god of the Golden Age—the harvest god—and of the products of the fruitful earth—the devourer of his children (Greek).

Moloch—the god of the Phœnicians—often identified with Kronos—to whom were made human sacrifices, particularly children.

Chemosh—the Moabite counterpart of Moloch—also identified with the Syrian Baal.

Baal—"Lord," the generic name for the principal god of the Canaanite and Phœnician worship—including Moloch, &c.

Bes—an early Egyptian deity—with brutal and slaughtering attributes—referable to an early stage of earth-worship.

Artemis—the Diana of the Ephesians—older than Greek my-thology, and originally the residing spirit of an aërolite—a nature goddess of fertility, requiring human sacrifices.

Saturn—the god of the Golden Age—the harvest god, and of fer-tility (Roman).

Set—the national god of the Hykshos dynasties in Egypt, the shepherd kings from Syria—afterwards the Egyptian personification of evil.

Seth—the son of Adam—by some identified as the original of Set.

INDEX.

THE END.